JAPANESE MADE EASY

$8.25

JAPANESE
MADE EASY

by
TAZUKO AJIRO MONANE, Ph.D.

CHARLES E. TUTTLE COMPANY
Rutland, Vermont and Tokyo, Japan

REPRESENTATIVES

For Continental Europe:
BOXERBOOKS, INC., *Zurich*

For the British Isles:
PRENTICE-HALL INTERNATIONAL, INC., *London*

For Australasia:
BOOK WISE (AUSTRALIA) PTY. LTD.
104-108 Sussex Street, Sydney 2000

Published by the Charles E. Tuttle Company, Inc.
of Rutland, Vermont & Tokyo, Japan
with editorial offices at
Suido 1-chome, 2-6, Bunkyo-ku, Tokyo

Library of Congress Catalog Card No. 79–6482
International Standard Book No. 0-8048 1219-5

First printing, 1979
Twelfth printing, 1987

Printed in Japan

─── TABLE OF CONTENTS ───

Acknowledgments............................... 9

Study Suggestions.............................. 11

Pronunciation 17

LESSON 1 23
  Situation 1: Ordering at a coffee shop   24
  Situation 2: Ordering at a bar   26
  Situation 3: Ordering at a restaurant   28
  Situation 4: Shopping at a department store   30

LESSON 2 34
  Situation 1: Letting others know what you want   34
  Situation 2: Asking questions and saying yes   41
  Situation 3: Saying no   44
  Situation 4: Asking "What?" and "Which one?"   46
  Situation 5: Asking "Where?"   50
  Situation 6: Eating at a *sushi* shop   51

LESSON 3 53
  Situation 1: Asking "Where?" and "Which way?"   53
  Situation 2: Asking what it is when you don't know   59
  Situation 3: Finding out what it is (and isn't)   62
  Situation 4: Asking about the family   65

LESSON 4 71
  Situation 1: Making suggestions   71
  Situation 2: Asking for suggestions   75
  Other Useful Verbs   79

LESSON 5 81
  Situation 1: Describing things   81
  The Conjugation of Adjectives   85
  Situation 2: Describing things *(continued)*   89
  Situation 3: Talking about this and that   93
  Situation 4: Using another kind of descriptive word   98
  Situation 5: Determining likes and dislikes   102

LESSON 6 106
  Situation 1: Handling money   107
  Situation 2: Buying tickets at a movie theater   111
  Situation 3: Buying tickets at a train station   113
  Situation 4: Buying stamps at a post office   114
  Situation 5: Keeping track of the time   116
  Situation 6: Understanding telephone numbers   120

LESSON 7 122
  Situation 1: Telling what you do or will do   123
  Situation 2: Telling what you did do   124
  Situation 3: Telling what you don't or didn't do   127
  The Japanese Verb   128

LESSON 8 133
  Situation 1: Buying fruit   133
  Situation 2: Buying vegetables   136
  Situation 3: Counting people   140
  Situation 4: Keeping track of the time   141

LESSON 9 150
  Situation 1: Making requests and offers   150
  Situation 2: Requesting things at a department store 152

Situation 3: Giving directions to a taxi driver   156
Situation 4: Making sure you understand and are
   understood   157
Situation 5: Seeking advice   159
Situation 6: Doing what the teacher tells you   160
Situation 7: Being very polite   160
Situation 8: Going to the beauty parlor or the
   barber   161
The Verb *-te* Form   164

LESSON 10 166
Situation 1: Greeting your friends   166
Situation 2: Greeting your friends *(continued)*   168
Situation 3: Rising to the occasion   171
Situation 4: Eating at someone else's home   174

Appendixes 177
1. Supplementary Vocabulary   177
2. Commonly Seen Words for Recognition   181
3. False Friends   184
4. Summary of Verb Conjugation   186

Glossary...............................189

Indexes 199
Grammar Discussions   199
Vocabulary Lists   201

—— ACKNOWLEDGMENTS ——

I should like to express my warm thanks most of all to my students, who have taught me the importance of placing in real-life situations each language pattern they learn. Their interest and motivation to learn when language comes situationally alive has been a major inspiration for me in preparing this book.

I am deeply indebted to Mrs. Pamela Miller for her help with the initial editing. The ideas, suggestions, and encouragement of my husband, Dr. Joseph Monane, have been a constant source of support. Finally, I should like to express my appreciation to the Charles E. Tuttle Company, whose receptivity to the format of this book has been a warm and gratifying experience.

───── STUDY SUGGESTIONS ─────

Japanese Made Easy is a basic, do-it-yourself guide to the Japanese language and is designed for persons living in or going to Japan who have never studied Japanese before. Obviously, living or traveling in Japan is itself not the secret of learning Japanese—many foreigners live in Japan a long time and except for a few words learn very little about its language. The important thing will be your motivation to learn. Whether you go to Japan as a tourist, student, or businessperson, whether you use this book before or after your arrival in Japan, what could provide better motivation than knowing that a familiarity with the Japanese language (and with the culture it reflects) will help make your stay in Japan much richer and much more interesting?

If you have the good fortune to know a Japanese person, he or she will surely make your learning even easier—especially when you study pronunciation. But don't be discouraged if you have no "live model" to learn from. By following the simple suggestions given here you will be able to come out with good, understandable Japanese on your own. Here are some ideas, then, for how you can get the most out of this book.

Situations. This book contains ten lessons, and within each lesson are several situations, each situation being one that you will actually encounter in Japan. Because the vocabulary, sentence patterns, explanations, and practice sections all work together to present the basics of the Japanese language in the context of a single situation, each situation section should be studied as a complete unit. The introduction of new language patterns within common situations is a basic principle that helps all learners, and it should help you develop a real feel for the material you study.

As your confidence grows through mastering the basic patterns provided for you, you will discover that the patterns are applicable in many more situations than those covered in this book. This book, therefore, does not attempt to cover all possible situations. Though you should, in the beginning, confine yourself to the material in each lesson, try later on to make up new situations on your own to see if you can handle them in Japanese.

Vocabulary Lists. The words used in each lesson plus other important words that will be good to know are introduced in the vocabulary lists. Depending on the time you can spend, choose the words you feel will be of most use to you. Go over the vocabulary lists often and try to make up sentences of your own. Just learning the words themselves will not be of great help to you. Remember that words are almost always used in sentences!

The supplementary vocabulary (Appendix 1) will give you some additional words you can use to help strengthen your speaking and comprehension skills.

Sentence Patterns. Devote most of your study to sentence patterns. The ones I have selected for you here are the core of the Japanese language. They are the building-blocks for a solid foundation onto which you can add, for each sentence pattern can be used in many different ways.

So approach each sentence pattern with patience. Practice it thoroughly before going on in the book. Use it as often as you can as a base for longer utterances of several sentences so that you avoid the choppy style that comes from using a sentence in isolation.

Sentence patterns throughout are numbered for your convenience. You will find the related forms of a basic sentence pattern marked A, B, or C. For example, 30A, 30B, and 30C are not three new sentence patterns but simply variations of Sentence Pattern 30. Studying these as a group will make your learning a good deal easier.

Explanations and Vocabulary Notes. These will help you see how the Japanese language operates and will point out its relation to certain features of Japanese culture. Generally, only basic, easily understood information is given here.

Practice Sections. These form a part of each lesson. But in addition, whenever you learn a new sentence pattern, try to practice it from several angles. For example:

1. See whether you can carry on dialogues with yourself. Play both persons' roles in these conversations. Even better, try to find a partner who will do this with you.

2. See whether you can ask questions in Japanese. Tape these questions on a tape recorder and then try to answer them in Japanese.

3. See whether you can describe the things around you.

4. See whether you can express what you're going to do, what you've done, what you usually do, and so on.

If you're resourceful when doing the above, it can be fun as well as a good way to learn.

Review. Before you go on to each new lesson be sure to go over what you've learned so that you know it thoroughly. Look at the vocabulary lists often. Repeat sentences to yourself while driving your car or while riding the bus or subway. If you're studying in Japan, find social situations in which you can use your Japanese. Be outgoing. Ask directions, even when you know the right way to go.

Lesson 10. A group of useful, everyday expressions (greetings and the like) is given in Lesson 10. These expressions have been placed here because they are most often idiomatic, specialized phrases that need to be memorized. But there is no reason for you to wait until you reach Lesson 10 before you begin to learn or use them. You might study Situation 1 of Lesson 10 along with Lessons 1 and 2, Situation 2 of Lesson 10 along with Lessons 3 and 4, and so on. Studying Lesson 10 this way will reduce the amount of material to memorize at one time, and it will give you many helpful expressions to use (and recognize when others use them) early in your learning.

Few foreigners in Japan take the trouble to become fluent in Japanese. Don't be surprised, then, if you find many Japanese people, pleased with your efforts, complimenting you even when you've achieved what you know to be a bare minimum of competence. Don't be spoiled by this and be content to stop where you are in your learning. Accept the morale-boost this kind of compliment can bring, but let your reach always exceed your present grasp so that you can continue to advance in your conversational skills.

Going to Japanese movies, watching Japanese TV programs, eavesdropping on conversations in Japanese (difficult to do, but when you can do it successfully you've really learned!), starting conversations with Japanese people (don't hesitate to do this; you'll find that Japanese will often initiate conversations in English with you)—all of these will be helpful to you. And don't be afraid of making mistakes. Japanese people will never ridicule you or make you feel embarrassed.

After completing this book you will find yourself able to shop, order drinks and meals, buy tickets, travel, and generally make yourself understood anywhere in Japan. You will be able to explore Japan on your own instead of being totally dependent on tours and planned excursions, and this will bring you many gratifying experiences you might otherwise miss. What's more, by completing this book you will have demonstrated that you have the ability to be a serious student of Japanese, and you will be in a good position to continue your study should you wish.

Many Westerners think Oriental languages are very difficult to learn. I hope that through this simple, easy-to-use guide to the Japanese language I may reach some readers who have had that feeling and help them realize that it is not so.

Good luck! Your diligence will help you understand not only the language but also the people and culture of Japan. I think you'll find they're worth the effort.

—TAZUKO AJIRO MONANE

University of Hawaii at Hilo

PRONUNCIATION

Pronunciation of Japanese is relatively easy. Once you acquire basic knowledge about Japanese sounds and master them with the help of a native speaker or with the help of recorded materials, you will not have much difficulty.

There are five vowels in Japanese. In this book these vowels are written: *a, i, u, e,* and *o.*

> *a*—like the *a* in *ha, ha!*
> *i*—like the *i* in *Bali*
> *u*—like the *u* in *June,* but shorter in length
> *e*—like the *e* in *pet*
> *o*—like the *o* in *colt*

Long and Short Vowels. Long vowels are written in this book as *ā, ii, ū, ē,* and *ō.* Don't confuse these with what are called long vowels in English. In Japanese, a long vowel is sustained twice as long as a short one, but the sound of the vowel remains the same. Therefore, it is often the length of the vowel that distinguishes one word from another. Note the important difference in meaning made by the short and long vowels in the following pairs.

obasan — aunt	*obāsan* — grandmother
ojisan — uncle	*ojiisan* — grandfather
kuki — stem	*kūki* — air
e — picture	*ē* — yes
oku — to put	*ōku* — plenty

Syllables. Japanese think of their words as being composed of syllables, each syllable taking one beat. A Japanese syllable may be any one of the following:

1. One short vowel only: *a, i, u, e, o.*
2. The first or second half of any long vowel *(ā, ii, ū, ē, ō).* Therefore, one long vowel equals two syllables.
3. A consonant + a vowel:

ka, ki, ku, ke, ko	*ga, gi, gu, ge, go*
sa, shi, su, se, so	*za, ji, zu, ze, zo*
ta, chi, tsu, te, to	*da, de, do*
na, ni, nu, ne, no	*ba, bi, bu, be, bo*
ha, hi, fu, he, ho	*pa, pi, pu, pe, po*
ma, mi, mu, me, mo	*ja, ju, jo*
ya, yu, yo	*wa*
ra, ri, ru, re, ro	

4. The consonant *n* (when not attached to a vowel). This syllable only appears:
(a) at the end of a word: *hon* — book
(b) in the middle of a word:
   (i) when followed by a consonant: *konnichi wa* — hello
   (ii) when followed by a vowel or *y:*

> *kin-en* — no smoking
> *un-yū* — transportation

Failure to pronounce the sounds exactly as marked by the hyphen may change the meaning of the word.

kin-en — no smoking   *kinen* — commemoration

shin-in — new member(s)   *shinin* — dead persons

The consonant *n* will be written *m* before the sounds *b, m,* and *p*.

sambyaku — three hundred

samman — thirty thousand

sampo — a walk

5. A combination of sounds: a consonant + the consonant *y* (or *h*) + a vowel:

kya, kyu, kyo	*mya, myu, myo*
sha, shu, sho	*rya, ryu, ryo*
cha, chu, cho	*gya, gyu, gyo*
nya, nyu, nyo	*bya, byu, byo*
hya, hyu, hyo	*pya, pyu, pyo*

6. The first consonant (only the first) of certain double consonants: *kk, ss, ssh, tt, tch, tts, pp*. Failure to give a full beat to this syllable may change the meaning of the word.

shitte — knowing	*shite* — doing
kitte — a stamp	*kite* — coming
issho — together	*isho* — last will
hikkaku — to scratch	*hikaku* — comparison
matchi — a match	*machi* — town
itta — went	*ita* — board, plank

Pronunciation of Consonants

1. The Japanese *r* seems to give the most trouble to speakers of other languages. If you pronounce *ra, ri, ru, re,*

and *ro* with exactly the same *r* as in English, you will not produce the correct Japanese sound. The Japanese *r* resembles a combination of the English *r* and *l*. So, relax your tongue and first practice saying *la, li, lu, le,* and *lo*. Next, close the lips more, hold them fairly steady, and pronounce the same sounds without rolling your tongue. You will be able to produce the correct Japanese *ra, ri, ru, re,* and *ro* that way.

2. The Japanese *f* as in *Fuji-san,* "Mt. Fuji," is very different from the English *f* in which you touch the lower lip with the upper teeth to get the sound. In Japanese, this is not done. The Japanese *f* is pronounced more like the English *h*.

3. The Japanese final *n* in such words as *hon,* "book," and *Nihon* or *Nippon,* "Japan," is a little different from the English final *n* in which the tongue touches the palate just behind the upper teeth, as in "one" and "ten." The Japanese final *n* is nasalized and more relaxed; the tongue does not touch the upper palate.

4. All other consonants should be pronounced as they are in English.

Pronunciation of Syllables. You must learn to pronounce each syllable clearly and with the same amount of stress. Each syllable must be equal in length. Note the number of syllables in the examples below. Remember, each syllable gets one beat, so a long vowel gets counted as two syllables. Give one beat to the consonant *n* and to the first consonant of the double consonant.

Ohayō.	*o-ha-yo-o* (4)	Good morning.
Ohayō gozaimasu.	*o-ha-yo-o-go-za-i-ma-su* (9)	Good morning.
Konnichi wa.	*ko-n-ni-chi-wa* (5)	Hello.

Komban wa.	*ko-m-ba-n-wa* (5)	Good evening.
hikkaku	*hi-k-ka-ku* (4)	to scratch

Don't put a heavy stress on any syllable. Particularly avoid the "potato" accent (a heavy stress on the second syllable of a three-syllable word) and the "macaroni" accent (a heavy stress on the third syllable of a four-syllable word). Practice the following proper names.

Matsui	Hashimoto
Nakao	Matsumoto
Tanaka	Takahashi
Yamada	Yamanaka

Remember: keep each syllable clear, equal in length, and even in stress.

Phrasing. In English, a preposition such as "in," "for," "of," or "at" and the noun or noun phrase that follows it are usually pronounced as a single unit: "in the ocean," "during my vacation," "of the company," "at seven o'clock." In Japanese, a particle (which often follows a noun) is pronounced as a part of the noun or noun phrase that precedes it. In the following sentences, a slash indicates the correct phrasing.

Kōhii o / kudasai.	Please give me a cup of coffee.
Sukiyaki ga / tabetai desu.	I want to eat *sukiyaki*.
Nara e / ikitai desu.	I want to go to Nara.

If you get used to this phrasing, you can perceive each of the three sentences above as comprising two units rather than three—which makes your learning much easier. (Think how easy it is to learn telephone numbers when you think of them not as seven separate digits but as two units—three digits plus four digits, as in 661–3561.)

This phrasing rule is one of the most important in Japanese. In the numbered sentence-pattern models you will be studying, the phrasing is clearly marked with a slash. You need not always pause while speaking, but if you do, make sure that the pause comes where it is marked in the sentence patterns in this book. Your Japanese will sound much more natural to Japanese ears.

LESSON 1

Many words borrowed from other languages (mostly English) are used frequently in Japanese. Several of these will be introduced in this lesson to give you an immediate working vocabulary that you can easily retain and use with confidence in many situations. These borrowed words will also give you practice in Japanese pronunciation.

It is absolutely essential to practice these Japanese borrowed words with the correct Japanese pronunciation. As Jack Seward* points out, the average citizen of Japan, upon hearing a Westerner (who is usually presumed to be an American) having difficulty speaking Japanese, often attempts to give that foreigner a helping hand by injecting as many borrowed words as he can into his own speech. The result is generally disastrous. This kindness would be beneficial if the borrowed words were used and pronounced in Japanese as they are used and pronounced in the language from which they were borrowed. Unfortunately, they seldom are, and the Westerner is more confused than ever.

Let's look at some situations in which these borrowed words are frequently used.

---

* Jack Seward, *Japanese in Action* (New York: Walker/Weatherhill, 1969), p. 98.

▣ Situation 1: Ordering at a coffee shop

Coffee shops or tea rooms, called *kissaten,* are numerous in Japan and are very popular places to meet friends and relax. You can order all kinds of soft drinks, desserts, and even light-lunch items such as sandwiches there.

VOCABULARY

aisu kōhii	ice coffee
aisukuriimu	ice cream
aisukuriimu sōda	ice cream soda
appuru pai	apple pie
chokorēto sēki	chocolate shake
hamu sandoitchi (hamu sando)*	ham sandwich
jūsu	juice
kēki	cake
kōhii	coffee
Kokakōra	Coca-Cola
kokoa	cocoa
mikkusu sandoitchi (mikkusu sando)	combination sandwich (usually, ham, cheese, egg, and tomato)
miruku	milk
orenji jūsu	orange juice
pai	pie
pan (from Portuguese *pão*)	bread
remonēdo	lemonade
sandoitchi (sando)	sandwich
sōda	soda
tomato jūsu	tomato juice

The first sentence pattern shows you the simplest way to ask for something in Japanese. It consists of the item (a

---

* A Japanese word in parentheses after the main entry is an alternate form or a word of the same meaning but of less frequent occurrence.

noun) you want, a particle, and a word meaning "please." Look carefully at the sentence pattern that follows.

Sentence Pattern 1

NOUN o / kudasai.   Please give me NOUN.

Kōhii o kudasai.
Please give me coffee.
Jūsu o kudasai.
Please give me juice.
Kēki o kudasai.
Please give me cake.
Aisukuriimu o kudasai.
Please give me ice cream.
Kokoa o kudasai.
Please give me cocoa.
Chokorēto sēki o kudasai.
Please give me (a) chocolate shake.

In any situation that involves buying or shopping, *kudasai* can mean "Please bring (me)," "Please sell (me)," or "Please give (me)." The *o* in *Kōhii o kudasai* is called a particle. It has no meaning in itself but indicates that the word preceding is the direct object in the sentence. Other particles will be introduced later.

There are no articles like "a" or "the" in Japanese. Although in English you tend to say, "Please give me *some* ice cream," Japanese usually just say, "Please give me ice cream."

PRACTICE

1. Practice the following dialogue. What the waitress says is

included primarily for your recognition, since you will hear it often in coffee shops and other places serving the public.

WAITRESS:

Nani ni shimashō ka? [*or*]	What shall I bring you? [*or*]
Nani ni nasaimasu ka?	What are you going to have?

CUSTOMER:

Kōhii o kudasai.	Please give me (some) coffee.
Appuru pai o kudasai.	Please give me (a piece of) apple pie.
Aisukuriimu o kudasai.	Please give me (some) ice cream.
Kokakōra o kudasai.	Please give me (a) Coca-Cola.
Miruku o kudasai.	Please give me (some) milk.
Orenji jūsu o kudasai.	Please give me (some) orange juice.

2. See if you can order the following items.

(a) coffee
(b) sandwich
(c) lemonade
(d) ice cream soda
(e) Coca-Cola

ANSWERS: (a) *Kōhii o kudasai.* (b) *Sandoitchi o kudasai.* (c) *Remonēdo o kudasai.* (d) *Aisukuriimu sōda o kudasai.* (e) *Kokakōra o kudasai.*

◈ Situation 2: Ordering at a bar

VOCABULARY

biiru	beer
burandē	brandy
jin fuizu	gin fizz
kakuteru	cocktail
ramu	rum
Sukotchi uisukii	Scotch whiskey
uisukii	whiskey
uisukii sawā	whiskey sour
uokka	vodka

Useful Expressions:

mizuwari de	with water and ice
sutorēto de	straight

Vocabulary Note: Mizuwari is a native Japanese word. The *de* in *mizuwari de* and *sutorēto de* is a particle that indicates the style of the drink, or how it is to be made. These phrases can be inserted into Sentence Pattern 1.

Sukotchi uisukii o kudasai.	Please give me a Scotch.
Sukotchi uisukii o mizuwari de kudasai.	Please give me a Scotch with water and ice.

A sentence like the one immediately above has two particles. One, the particle *o*, shows what you wish to receive. The other, the particle *de*, here shows "how" you want to receive it. The particle *de* has other uses, some of which will be covered later in this book.

PRACTICE

1. Practice using Sentence Pattern 1. Note that the bartender's question below is the same as the waitress's on page 26 but the translation is different. What is important to learn is the intention of the speaker, and this is something that is often not clearly shown in a literal translation. Note these differences as you work through this book.

BARTENDER:

Nani ni shimashō ka?	What shall I make for you?

CUSTOMER:

Uisukii sawā o kudasai.	Please give me a whiskey sour.
Biiru o kudasai.	Please give me a beer.
Sukotchi uisukii o mizuwari de kudasai.	Please give me a Scotch with water and ice.
Uisukii o sutorēto de kudasai.	Please give me a straight Scotch.

2. See if you can order the following items in a bar.

(a) beer   (c) brandy
(b) Scotch with water   (d) Scotch straight
   and ice

ANSWERS: (a) *Biiru o kudasai.* (b) *Sukotchi uisukii o mizuwari de kudasai.* (c) *Burandē o kudasai.* (d) *Sukotchi uisukii o sutorēto de kudasai.*

◈ Situation 3: Ordering at a restaurant

VOCABULARY

yōshoku	Western-style food

Main Dishes:

bifuteki (biifusutēki)	beefsteak
biifu karē	beef curry
biifu shichū	beef stew
chikin karē	chicken curry
hambāgā	hamburger
karē raisu	curry rice
katsuretsu	cutlet
korokke	croquette
rōsuto biifu	roast beef
rōsuto pōku	roast pork
sarada	salad
shurimpu karē	shrimp curry
sūpu	soup

Breakfast Items:

bēkon	bacon
hamu	ham
omuretsu	omelet
sōsēji	sausage

To order two or more items, you need to know the Japanese expression that is equivalent to the English word "and." Though in English you say, "Give me A, B, C, and D," in Japanese you say, "Give me A and B and C and D."

"And" in Japanese is expressed by the particle *to*. The function of *to* in Japanese is to connect words or phrases, but not clauses or sentences.

─────── **Sentence Pattern 1A** ───────

NOUN to NOUN o / kudasai.   Please give me NOUN
                               and NOUN.

NOUN to NOUN to NOUN o /   Please give me NOUN,
kudasai.   NOUN, and NOUN.

───────────────

Hambāgā to kōhii o kudasai.
Please give me a hamburger and coffee.
Omuretsu to jūsu to kōhii o kudasai.
Please give me an omelet, juice, and coffee.

PRACTICE

1. Practice the following dialogue.

WAITRESS:
Nani ni shimashō ka?   What shall I bring you?
CUSTOMER:
Biifu karē to sarada o   Please bring me beef curry and
kudasai.   salad.
Hambāgā to biiru o kudasai. Please bring me a hamburger
                               and a beer.
Sarada to miruku o kudasai. Please bring me a salad and
                               some milk.

2. See if you can order two items in a coffee shop or a bar.
   (a) coffee and cake   (d) lemonade and a piece of
   (b) milk and ham sandwich   apple pie
   (c) coffee and salad   (e) gin fizz and beer

ANSWERS: (a) *Kōhii to kēki o kudasai.* (b) *Miruku to hamu sando o kudasai.* (c) *Kōhii to sarada o kudasai.* (d) *Remonēdo to appuru pai kudasai.* (e) *Jin fuizu to biiru o kudasai.*

◈ Situation 4: Shopping at a department store

VOCABULARY

doresu	dress
fuirumu	roll of film
hankachi	handkerchief
kādegan	cardigan
kamera	camera
karā terebi	color television set
kōto	coat
nekutai	necktie
rajio	radio
reinkōto (renkōto)	raincoat
rekōdo	record
sētā	sweater
shatsu	undershirt
sukāfu	scarf
sukāto	skirt
surakkusu	slacks
sutereo	stereo set
sūtsu	suit
tabako	pack of cigarettes
tēpu rekōdā	tape recorder
terebi	television set
waishatsu	dress shirt

Vocabulary Note: The word *shatsu* usually refers only to an undershirt. If you refer to a long-sleeved dress shirt of the sort worn with a suit, use the word *waishatsu*. Depending on the type of shirt, there are also such words as *supōtsu shatsu,* "sports shirt," *aroha shatsu,* "aloha shirt," and so on.

If you use the word *pantsu* to indicate a pair of slacks, you may produce giggles from a Japanese person. *Pantsu* generally means "underwear." The Japanese word for men's "pants" is *zubon.*

When shopping in Japan, you may not always know the

correct word for the item you wish to buy. In such cases, of course, you can just point to the item and use words for "this" or "that." Sometimes, though, you will know the Japanese word for the item but will wish to specify which among several is the particular one you want.

In English, the sentences "Please give me this" and "Please give me this camera" both use the same word, "this," to specify the item you want. In Japanese, however, the noun and adjective forms of "this" (and "that") are different. Look at the following sentence pattern.

Sentence Pattern 1B

Kore o / kudasai.	Please give this to me.
Sore o	it
Are o	that
Kono NOUN o / kudasai.	Please give me this NOUN.
Sono NOUN o	the
Ano NOUN o	that

Kore o kudasai.
Please give this (these) to me.
Kono kamera o kudasai.
Please give me this (these) camera(s) (close to me).
Sono kamera o kudasai.
Please give me that (the, those) camera(s) (close to you).
Ano kamera o kudasai.
Please give me that (those) camera(s) (some distance from you and me).

Kore, sore, and *are* take the place of the noun, just as an English pronoun does. But they are unlike English pronouns in that they have the same form whether the meaning you intend is singular or plural.

Kono, sono, and *ano* cannot be used without a following noun. Note, too, that Japanese nouns are unlike most English nouns in that they normally take the same form whether singular or plural.

Use *kore* and *kono* to indicate an object closer to you, the speaker.

Use *sore* and *sono* to indicate an object closer to your listener.

Use *are* and *ano* to indicate an object some distance from both you and your listener.

PRACTICE

1. Practice the following dialogue.

CLERK:

Nani o sashiagemashō ka? [*or*] What shall I bring you? [*or*]
Nani ni shimashō ka? What can I do for you?

CUSTOMER:

Sono reinkōto o kudasai. Please sell me the raincoat (which is close to you).

Kono sukāfu o kudasai. Please sell me this scarf.
Ano sētā o kudasai. Please sell me that sweater.
Kore o kudasai. Please sell me this.
Sore o kudasai. Please sell me that (which is close to you).

2. See if you can shop in a department store by specifying which among several is the particular one you want.

   (a)   this necktie   (d)   the camera that is close to
   (b)   that scarf   the clerk
   (c)   this roll of film   (e)   that sweater

ANSWERS: (a) *Kono nekutai o kudasai.*   (b) *Ano sukāfu o kudasai.*

(c) *Kono fuirumu o kudasai.*   (d) *Sono kamera o kudasai.*   (e) *Ano sētā o kudasai.*

~~~~~~~~Sentence Patterns Covered in This Lesson~~~~~~~~

1.   NOUN o / kudasai.
1A.   NOUN to NOUN o / kudasai.
      NOUN to NOUN to NOUN o / kudasai.
1B.   Kore o / kudasai.
      Sore o
      Are o
      Kono NOUN o / kudasai.
      Sono NOUN o
      Ano NOUN o

LESSON 2

In Lesson 1 you were introduced to words in Japanese borrowed from other languages. In this lesson you will learn some native Japanese words and the verbs "to eat," "to drink," "to see," "to buy," and "to go." The sentence patterns here will teach you how to express your most basic needs as a traveler in Japan and, just as important, how to find out what your Japanese friends want to do. The lesson will end at a *sushi* shop, where you will have the chance to select and sample some of the many kinds of fish used in this exquisite cuisine.

◈ Situation 1: Letting others know what you want

VOCABULARY

Useful Terms:

ippin ryōri	one-course meal; dishes a la carte
o-kanjō	bill, check
teishoku	main dish served with soup, rice, pickles, and salad; full-course dinner
washoku	Japanese-style food

Food Items:

go-han	cooked rice; meal
misoshiru	soup made from soybean paste

mizutaki	simmered chicken, usually cooked at your table
nigirizushi	small rolls of cooked, vinegared rice with pieces of fresh seafood on top
awabi	abalone
ebi	shrimp
ika	squid, cuttlefish
ikura	salmon roe
maguro	tuna
tako	octopus
toro	belly flesh of tuna (considered a delicacy)
uni	sea urchin
norimaki (**makizushi**)	small rolls of cooked rice with vegetables, wrapped in tissue-thin seaweed *(nori)*
o-sashimi	slices of raw fish, served with soy sauce and *wasabi,* "green horseradish"
o-sushi	vinegared rice topped with raw fish or wrapped in tissue-thin seaweed *(nori)*
oyako domburi	rice with chicken and eggs (*Oyako* literally means "parents and children.")
rāmen	Chinese-style noodles in soup
shabushabu	simmered beef, usually cooked at your table
soba	thin wheat noodles
sukiyaki	beef with vegetables, usually cooked at your table
tempura	batter-dipped and deep-fried shrimp, fish, and vegetables
teppan-yaki	meat and vegetables, usually cooked at your table on an iron grill
tonkatsu	pork cutlet
udon	thick wheat noodles
kitsune udon	noodles with fried *tōfu* (bean curd)
tempura udon	noodles with *tempura*
unagi domburi	broiled marinated eels on cooked rice

unagi teishoku	broiled marinated eels served with soup, rice, and pickles
yakitori	charcoal-grilled chicken, chicken liver, and green onions on a bamboo stick

Drinks:

agari	Japanese green tea (This word is usually used only in *sushi* shops.)
nomimono	something to drink
o-cha	Japanese green tea (This word can be used anywhere.)
o-hiya	cold water (This word is used in Japanese-style restaurants.)
o-kōcha	English tea
o-mizu	water (This word can be used anywhere.)
o-sake	Japanese rice wine, sakè

Clothing:

geta	wooden clogs
happi	*happi* coat (a colorful, waistlength coat)
kimono	kimono
obi	sash worn with kimono
yukata	summer cotton kimono
zōri	Japanese-style sandals

Entertainment:

Bunraku	puppet play
eiga	movie
Kabuki	Kabuki play
Nō	Noh play

Arts and Handicrafts:

byōbu	folding screens
hanga	woodblock print
katana	sword
kokeshi	Japanese wooden doll
mingeihin	folkcraft objects
sensu	paper folding fan
shinju	pearl

sumie	brush painting
takeseihin (takezaiku)	bamboo craft objects, bamboo products
ukiyoe	a particular genre of woodblock print
yakimono	pottery

Vocabulary Note: The prefixes *go-* and *o-* in *go-han, o-sashimi, o-cha, o-mizu,* and so on, make the noun more polite to Japanese ears. Male speakers sometimes omit the prefixes, but female speakers almost always use them. In some cases, for example in *go-han,* the prefix cannot be dropped. You are advised to use only the polite form, which is always correct.

When a noun is used as the second part of a compound word, its pronunciation often changes slightly; e.g., in *nigirizushi* the *s* of *sushi* changes to *z*.

The word *o-cha* refers to Japanese green tea; *o-kōcha* (literally, red tea) refers to English black tea. *O-hiya* is a special word for cold water, and it is used in Japanese-style restaurants, *sushi* shops, etc.

The *ei* in *eiga,* "movie," is pronounced more like *ē,* as are the *ei* spellings in other Japanese words.

The next two sentence patterns will be of great help to you in restaurants, stores, and train stations. By mastering these patterns and the new verbs they introduce, you will be able to satisfy most of your basic needs as a traveler in Japan.

More detailed notes on verb conjugation will be presented later in this book. Looking at Sentence Patterns 2 and 3, however, we can make a few initial remarks about verbs and about Japanese sentence construction.

First, note that stating the subject (I, in this case) is usually not necessary in Japanese when the subject is obvious from the context of the sentence. Also, *Tabetai desu* by itself is a complete sentence.

Sentence Pattern 2

NOUN ga / VERB-INFINITIVE +   I'd like to VERB NOUN.
-tai desu.

Sukiyaki ga tabetai desu.
I'd like to eat *sukiyaki.*
Biiru ga nomitai desu.
I'd like to drink beer.
Kamera ga kaitai desu.
I'd like to buy a camera.
Kabuki ga mitai desu.
I'd like to see a Kabuki play.

Sentence Pattern 3

PLACE e / ikitai desu.   I'd like to go to PLACE.

Kyōto e ikitai desu.
I'd like to go to Kyōto.
Nihon e ikitai desu.
I'd like to go to Japan.

In Japanese, the words carrying a verbal meaning usually go at the very end of the sentence. In the examples above, the *-tai desu* ending expresses the meaning "would like to do" and is attached to what we will call the verb-infinitive form of the verb. This will be explained later, but for now, memorize the following verb-infinitives and note the *-tai desu* endings.

| eat | tabe- | **Tabetai desu.** | (I) would like to eat. |
| drink | nomi- | **Nomitai desu.** | (I) would like to drink. |

buy	**kai-**	**Kaitai desu.**	(I) would like to buy.
see	**mi-**	**Mitai desu.**	(I) would like to see.
go	**iki-**	**Ikitai desu.**	(I) would like to go.

The word *desu* here has no real function other than to make the phrase sound more polite to Japanese ears. (Another use of *desu* in the sense of English "is" or "are" will be shown later.) Thus, *Tabetai* means exactly the same thing as *Tabetai desu,* but it is more informal. Such informal expressions are most often used with family members or close friends. The matter is not so simple, however, and understanding when informal speech is appropriate requires more than a little knowledge of Japanese culture. A few informal forms are presented in this book because they are commonly used or show some important characteristics of Japanese words. But you are strongly advised to use only the polite forms of speech (the *desu* in *Tabetai desu,* the *o-* in *o-sake*) until you become more familiar with the language and the people.

In Lesson 1 you learned the sentence pattern NOUN *o kudasai,* "Please give me NOUN," in which the noun (the item requested) was followed by the particle *o*. In Sentence Pattern 2 in this lesson the particle *ga* is introduced as an object marker when the verb ends in *-tai desu.*

| **Biiru o kudasai.** | Please give me a beer. |
| **Biiru ga nomitai desu.** | I'd like to drink beer. |

Among the younger generation in Japan, the particle *o* instead of *ga* is coming into use in the *-tai desu* construction. Whichever you hear, though, the meaning is the same.

Sentence Pattern 3 shows the particle *e,* which expresses direction or destination.

PRACTICE

1. Practice saying the following short sentences.

(a) to eat

O-sushi ga tabetai desu.	I'd like to eat	sushi.
Sukiyaki		sukiyaki.
Tempura		tempura.

(b) to drink

Biiru ga nomitai desu.	I'd like to drink	beer.
Kōhii		coffee.
O-cha		tea.
Sūpu		soup.

(c) to buy

Kamera ga kaitai desu.	I'd like to buy a	camera.
Rajio		radio.
Rekōdo		record.

(d) to see

Bunraku ga mitai desu.	I'd like to see	a puppet play.
Eiga		a movie.
Kabuki		a Kabuki play.
Nō		a Noh play.
Terebi		television.

(e) to go

Hokkaidō e ikitai desu.	I'd like to go to	Hokkaidō.
Kyōto		Kyōto.
Nihon (Nippon)		Japan.
Ōsaka		Ōsaka.
Sapporo		Sapporo.

Vocabulary Note: In English you "eat" soup, while in Japanese you "drink" soup. This reflects different eating habits. In the West you use a soup spoon and do not lift the soup bowl. In Japan you hold the bowl (usually a piece of lacquerware) in the palm of the left hand, bring the soup bowl close to your mouth, and drink or sip the soup. Any item in the soup such as fish, vegetables, or *tōfu* may be eaten with the help of chopsticks. Good luck in picking up *tōfu* with chopsticks; it requires some skill. And just as a note, when you pick up an item of food with chopsticks, it's not necessary to take it all in at one gulp. It's quite proper to bite off just a small piece.

2. Practice Sentence Patterns 2 and 3 with the following words.

(a) to eat

bifuteki	**sukiyaki**
karē raisu	**tempura**
o-sashimi	**tonkatsu**
o-sushi	

(b) to drink

biiru	**o-mizu**
kōhii	**orenji jūsu**
o-cha	**o-sake**

(c) to buy

happi	**obi**
kamera	**yukata**
kimono	**zōri**

(d) to see

Bunraku	**Kabuki**
eiga	**Nō**

(e) to go

Hiroshima	**Nara**
Kōbe	**Okayama**
Nagasaki	**Ōsaka**
Tōkyō	**Sapporo**

◈ **Situation 2: Asking questions and saying yes**

So far you have been practicing statements. With these

statements, you can express certain basic needs, but your ability to communicate is still limited. By being able to ask questions and answer them, you will be able to achieve real two-way communication.

Sentence Pattern 2A

NOUN ga / VERB-INFINITIVE + -tai desu ka? Would you like to VERB NOUN?

O-sushi ga tabetai desu ka?
Would you like to eat *sushi?*
O-sake ga nomitai desu ka?
Would you like to drink sakè?
Kimono ga kaitai desu ka?
Would you like to buy a kimono?
Kabuki ga mitai desu ka?
Would you like to see a Kabuki play?

Sentence Pattern 3A

PLACE e / ikitai desu ka? Would you like to go to PLACE?

Nihon e ikitai desu ka?
Would you like to go to Japan?
Hawai e ikitai desu ka?
Would you like to go to Hawaii?

The particle *ka* used at the end of a sentence makes the sentence into a question. Notice that in forming questions in Japanese there is no inversion of word order as there is in English.

Sentence Pattern 4

Hai (Ē) / VERB-INFINITIVE +   Yes, I'd like to VERB.
-tai desu.

Hai (Ē), tabetai desu.
Yes, I'd like to eat (that).
Hai (Ē), nomitai desu.
Yes, I'd like to drink (that).
Hai (Ē), kaitai desu.
Yes, I'd like to buy (that).
Hai (Ē), mitai desu.
Yes, I'd like to see (that).
Hai (Ē), ikitai desu.
Yes, I'd like to go (there).

Hai, tabetai desu is a complete sentence. You need not mention the object, which is usually understood from the context of the sentence. In English, this response often takes the form, "Yes, I'd like to." Notice that in Japanese an appropriate verb must always be used. *Hai, tabetai desu* is comparable to the English "Yes, I'd like to eat (it, some, this, etc.)."

Hai, "yes," is a little more formal than *ē. Hai* (but not *ē*) is also used to respond when someone calls out your name.

PRACTICE

Try translating the following short dialogues using the sentence patterns in this lesson.
1. Would you like to eat *sukiyaki?*
   Yes, I'd like to eat some.
2. Would you like to drink a beer?
   Yes, I'd like to drink one.

3. Would you like to buy a camera?
   Yes, I'd like to buy one.
4. Would you like to watch television?
   Yes, I'd like to watch it.
5. Would you like to go to Japan?
   Yes, I'd like to go there.

ANSWERS: 1. *Sukiyaki ga tabetai desu ka?   Hai (Ē), tabetai desu.*
2. *Biiru ga nomitai desu ka?   Hai (Ē), nomitai desu.   3. Kamera ga kaitai desu ka?   Hai (Ē), kaitai desu.   4. Terebi ga mitai desu ka? Hai (Ē), mitai desu.   5. Nihon e ikitai desu ka?   Hai (Ē), ikitai desu.*

◈ Situation 3: Saying no

You have practiced answering questions affirmatively. Although the negative answers are somewhat more complicated, it's important to learn them. You wouldn't want literally to be someone who can't say no.

Sentence Pattern 5

Iie / VERB-INFINITIVE +   No, I wouldn't like to
   -taku arimasen.   VERB.

Iie, tabetaku arimasen.
No, I wouldn't like to eat that.
Iie, nomitaku arimasen.
No, I wouldn't like to drink that.
Iie, kaitaku arimasen.
No, I wouldn't like to buy that.
Iie, mitaku arimasen.
No, I wouldn't like to see that.
Iie, ikitaku arimasen.
No, I wouldn't like to go there.

In order to form the negative of the verb-form "would like to (do)," change the last letter -*i* in the affirmative -*tai* into -*ku* and add *arimasen*. Compare:

VERB-INFINITIVE + -**tai desu.**
VERB-INFINITIVE + -**taku arimasen.**

Tabetai desu.	I would like to eat.
Tabetaku arimasen.	I would not like to eat.

PRACTICE

Answer the following questions first with "yes" and then with "no."

1. **Nihon e ikitai desu ka?**
2. **Sukiyaki ga tabetai desu ka?**
3. **Biiru ga nomitai desu ka?**
4. **Kimono ga kaitai desu ka?**
5. **Kyōto e ikitai desu ka?**
6. **Eiga ga mitai desu ka?**
7. **Kabuki ga mitai desu ka?**
8. **Kamera ga kaitai desu ka?**
9. **O-sake ga nomitai desu ka?**
10. **O-sushi ga tabetai desu ka?**

YES	NO
1. Hai (Ē), ikitai desu.	Iie, ikitaku arimasen.
2. Hai (Ē), tabetai desu.	Iie, tabetaku arimasen.
3. Hai (Ē), nomitai desu.	Iie, nomitaku arimasen.
4. Hai (Ē), kaitai desu.	Iie, kaitaku arimasen.
5. Hai (Ē), ikitai desu.	Iie, ikitaku arimasen.
6. Hai (Ē), mitai desu.	Iie, mitaku arimasen.
7. Hai (Ē), mitai desu.	Iie, mitaku arimasen.
8. Hai (Ē), kaitai desu.	Iie, kaitaku arimasen.
9. Hai (Ē), nomitai desu.	Iie, nomitaku arimasen.
10. Hai (Ē), tabetai desu.	Iie, tabetaku arimasen.

❧ **Situation 4: Asking "What?" and "Which one?"**

The next sentence pattern will enable you to ask "What would you like to (do)?" and "Which (one) would you like to (do)?"

Sentence Pattern 2B

Nani ga / VERB-INFINITIVE + -tai desu ka? — What would you like to VERB?

Dore ga / VERB-INFINITIVE + -tai desu ka? — Which one would you like to VERB?

Nani ga tabetai desu ka?
What would you like to eat?
Nani ga nomitai desu ka?
What would you like to drink?
Nani ga kaitai desu ka?
What would you like to buy?
Nani ga mitai desu ka?
What would you like to see?

Dore ga tabetai desu ka?
Which one would you like to eat?
Dore ga nomitai desu ka?
Which one would you like to drink?
Dore ga kaitai desu ka?
Which one would you like to buy?
Dore ga mitai desu ka?
Which one would you like to see?

PRACTICE

Practice the following short dialogues.

Nani ga tabetai desu ka? — What would you like to eat?
O-sashimi ga tabetai desu. — I'd like to eat *sashimi*.

Nani ga nomitai desu ka?	What would you like to drink?
Kōhii ga nomitai desu.	I'd like to drink coffee.
Nani ga kaitai desu ka?	What would you like to buy?
Kamera ga kaitai desu.	I'd like to buy a camera.
Nani ga mitai desu ka?	What would you like to see?
Kabuki ga mitai desu.	I'd like to see a Kabuki play.
Dore ga tabetai desu ka?	Which one would you like to eat?
Kore ga tabetai desu.	I'd like to eat this.

(pointing to an item on the menu or in the shopwindow)

Dore ga nomitai desu ka?	Which one would you like to drink?
Sore ga nomitai desu.	I'd like to drink that.

(pointing to an item located near the listener)

Dore ga kaitai desu ka?	Which one would you like to buy?
Are ga kaitai desu.	I'd like to buy that.

(pointing to an item away from the speaker and the listener)

Dore ga mitai desu ka?	Which one would you like to see?
Kore ga mitai desu.	I'd like to see this one.

(pointing to an advertisement in the newspaper)

The next sentence pattern is Sentence Pattern 2B with only a slight change. The literal translation of Sentence Pattern 2C is "What and what (*or* which and which) would you like to eat (drink, buy, etc.)?" This expression is rarely used in English but is often used in Japanese when the speaker wishes to ask if there is more than one thing that his listener would like to do or have. The number of items in the answer is not necessarily limited to two, even though the question here uses *nani* and *dore* twice only.

Sentence Pattern 2C

Nani to nani ga / VERB-INFINITIVE + -tai desu ka?

What things would you like to VERB?

Dore to dore ga / VERB-INFINITIVE + -tai desu ka?

Which things would you like to VERB?

Nani to nani ga tabetai desu ka?
What things would you like to eat?
Nani to nani ga nomitai desu ka?
What things would you like to drink?
Nani to nani ga kaitai desu ka?
What things would you like to buy?
Nani to nani ga mitai desu ka?
What things would you like to see?

Dore to dore ga tabetai desu ka?
Which things would you like to eat?
Dore to dore ga nomitai desu ka?
Which things would you like to drink?
Dore to dore ga kaitai desu ka?
Which things would you like to buy?
Dore to dore ga mitai desu ka?
Which things would you like to see?

PRACTICE

1. **Nani to nani ga tabetai desu ka?**

   What (and what) would you like to eat?

   Bifuteki to sarada ga tabetai desu.

   I'd like to eat beefsteak and salad.

   Nani to nani ga kaitai desu ka?

   What (and what) would you like to buy?

Kimono to kamera to karā terebi ga kaitai desu.

I'd like to buy a kimono, a camera, and a color television set.

Nani to nani ga mitai desu ka?

What (and what) would you like to see?

Kabuki to Bunraku ga mitai desu.

I'd like to see a Kabuki play and a puppet play.

2. **Dore to dore ga** ⎰ **tabetai desu ka?**
   ⎪ **nomitai**
   ⎪ **kaitai**
   ⎱ **mitai**

Which things would you like to ⎰ eat?
   ⎪ drink?
   ⎪ buy?
   ⎱ see?

(Pointing to two items close to the speaker)
Kore to kore ga ⎰ **tabetai desu.**
   ⎪ **nomitai**
   ⎪ **kaitai**
   ⎱ **mitai**

I'd like to ⎰ eat these (this and this).
   ⎪ drink
   ⎪ buy
   ⎱ see

(Pointing to two items close to the listener)
Sore to sore ga ⎰ **tabetai desu.**
   ⎪ **nomitai**
   ⎪ **kaitai**
   ⎱ **mitai**

I'd like to ⎰ eat those (that and that).
   ⎪ drink
   ⎪ buy
   ⎱ see

(Pointing to two items at some distance)
Are to are ga ⌠ tabetai desu.
               nomitai
               kaitai
               ⌊ **mitai**
I'd like to ⌠ eat those over there (that and that).
        drink
        buy
        ⌊ see

◈ Situation 5: Asking "Where?"

Sentence Pattern 3B

Doko e / ikitai desu ka?   Where would you like to
                                  go?

Sentence Pattern 3C

Doko to doko e / ikitai   Where (and where) would
desu ka?   you like to go? [*or*]
                        To what places would you
                        like to go?

As with *nani* and *dore,* the number of places in the answer need not be limited to two, although the question here uses *doko* twice only.

PRACTICE

Practice the following dialogues.
Doko e ikitai desu ka?   Where would you like to go?
Nihon e ikitai desu.   I'd like to go to Japan.

Doko to doko e ikitai desu ka?   To what places would you
                                       like to go?

Kyōto to Nara e ikitai desu.	I'd like to go to Kyōto and Nara.
Doko to doko e ikitai desu ka?	Where (and where) would you like to go?
Hiroshima to Miyajima e ikitai desu.	I'd like to go to Hiroshima and Miyajima.

◈ Situation 6: Eating at a sushi shop

Instead of ordering a dish of *sushi* to be served at your table, it is sometimes more fun to sit at the counter, order individual *sushi* as you wish, and watch the skill with which it is made. Professional *sushi* makers are very proud of their speed and dexterity. Before you enter, try to find out the price the shop charges, since some shops are quite expensive.

Suppose a Japanese friend takes you out for *sushi*. The following will probably take place when you walk in the door and sit at the counter.

SUSHI MAKER:

Irasshaimase!	Welcome!

YOU AND YOUR FRIEND:

Komban wa. [*or*]	Good evening. [*or*]
Konnichi wa.	Good afternoon.

SUSHI MAKER:

Nani ni shimashō ka?	What shall I make for you?

YOUR FRIEND (will turn to you and say):

Nani to nani ga tabetai desu ka?	What things would you like to eat?

Practice, using the words under *nigirizushi* on page 35, answers to your friend's question like the following.

Awabi ga tabetai desu.	I'd like to eat abalone.
Uni to ikura ga tabetai desu.	I'd like to eat sea urchin and salmon roe.

Usually, if you go with a Japanese, he will order for you. The *sushi* maker will then make two small *nigirizushi* of each kind ordered. If you go to the *sushi* shop by yourself, order the various types of *nigirizushi* in the following way:

Ika o kudasai.	Please give me squid.
Tako o kudasai.	Please give me octopus.
Maguro o kudasai.	Please give me tuna.
Awabi o kudasai.	Please give me abalone.

If you don't know the name of the fish or prefer to pick whatever looks interesting from the case on the counter, just point to the item you want and say:

Kore o kudasai.	Please give me this.

To order hot tea while you are eating, ask for *agari*.

Agari o kudasai.	Please give me some tea.

When you have finished and are about to leave, ask for your bill as follows:

O-kanjō o kudasai.	May I have the bill, please?

Sentence Patterns Covered in This Lesson

2. NOUN ga / VERB-INFINITIVE + -tai desu.
2A. NOUN ga / VERB-INFINITIVE + -tai desu ka?
2B. Nani ga / VERB-INFINITIVE + -tai desu ka?
    Dore ga / VERB-INFINITIVE + -tai desu ka?
2C. Nani to nani ga / VERB-INFINITIVE + -tai desu ka?
    Dore to dore ga / VERB-INFINITIVE + -tai desu ka?
3. PLACE e / ikitai desu.
3A. PLACE e / ikitai desu ka?
3B. Doko e / ikitai desu ka?
3C. Doko to doko e / ikitai desu ka?
4. Hai (Ē) / VERB-INFINITIVE + -tai desu.
5. Iie / VERB-INFINITIVE + -taku arimasen.

—————— LESSON 3 ——————

In Lesson 2 you were introduced to questions using the words *nani, dore,* and *doko.* In this lesson you will learn a series of related sentence patterns that will increase your ability to ask what, which, and where questions. You will learn how to ask directions, how to ask for information about the things you see around you on the street or in a restaurant, and how to discover more about the Japanese people with whom you will be spending some of your time.

◈ Situation 1: Asking "Where?" and "Which way?"

VOCABULARY

Amerika Ryōjikan	American Consulate
Amerika Taishikan	American Embassy
annaijo	information desk
apāto	apartment building
basu no noriba (basu no teiryūjo)	bus stop
bijutsukan	art museum
biyōin	beauty salon
byōin	hospital
chikatetsu no eki (chikatetsu no noriba)	subway station
daigaku	university
eigakan	movie theater

eki	station
eki no baiten	station store, kiosk
gakkō	school
ginkō	bank
guriru	grill (in a Western-style hotel)
hikōjō, kūkō	airport
hon-ya	book store
hoteru	hotel
hoteru no shokudō	hotel dining room
kippu uriba	ticket counter
kōban (kōbansho)	police substation
koin rokkā	coin locker
kōshū denwa	public telephone
kusuriya (yakkyoku)	drug store
nimotsu ichiji azukarijo	baggage check room
o-tearai (toire)	toilet, bathroom
rihatsuten (bābā shoppu)	barber shop
ryokan	Japanese inn
shashin-ya	photo studio
shokudō	dining room, eating place
takushii noriba	taxi stand
toshokan	library
yūbinkyoku	post office

Vocabulary Note: Make sure to clearly distinguish between *byōin* and *biyōin*. *Byōin* means "hospital," and *biyōin* means "beauty salon." In the names of hospitals, banks, and other institutions, the proper name, as in English, always comes first: *Mitsubishi Ginkō,* "Mitsubishi Bank."

The word *hikōjō* is a general word for "airport." The word *kūkō* is often used with the name of the airport, as in *Narita Kūkō,* "Narita Airport."

The suffix *-ya* as in *shashin-ya* or *hon-ya* means "shop" or "stand."

Like English, Japanese has many words for "toilet." Among

LESSON 3 · 55

these are *o-tearai, toire* (borrowed from English), *o-benjo,* and *go-fujo. O-tearai* is the safest, most general form for you to use.

Instead of *rihatsuten,* the word *bābā shoppu* (from English "barber shop") is often used in Western-style hotels.

If you have just arrived or are in a strange part of town, you can use the following sentence patterns to get your bearings, find a place to eat, or make your way home.

Sentence Pattern 6

(Chotto sumimasen ga) / PLACE wa / doko desu ka? (Excuse me, but) where is PLACE?

(Chotto sumimasen ga) / PLACE wa / dochira desu ka? (Excuse me, but) which way is PLACE?

(Chotto sumimasen ga) o-tearai wa doko desu ka?
(Excuse me, but) where is the toilet?
(Chotto sumimasen ga) Tōkyō Eki wa doko desu ka?
(Excuse me, but) where is Tōkyō Station?
(Chotto sumimasen ga) chikatetsu no eki wa dochira desu ka?
(Excuse me, but) which way is the subway station?
(Chotto sumimasen ga) kōshū denwa wa dochira desu ka?
(Excuse me, but) which way is the public telephone?

In Sentence Pattern 6 the particle used is *wa. Wa* has several uses in Japanese, but the one most frequently shown in this book is its use as a topic marker; that is, *wa* shows what you are talking or asking about. In Sentence Pattern 6, the topic of the sentence—that is, the noun followed by *wa*—corresponds to the subject in English.

Chotto sumimasen ga is used like the English "Excuse me, but . . ." to make one's questioning of a stranger less abrupt.

Desu was used earlier to make a sentence like *Tabetai desu* more polite. In this lesson, the meaning of *desu* is like that of the English "is" or "are."

Sentence Pattern 7

NOUN OF DIRECTION desu.   It's DIRECTION (here, this way, that way, etc.).

Koko desu.
It's here.
Soko desu.
It's there.
Asoko desu.
It's over there.
Kochira (kotchi) desu.
It's this way.
Sochira (sotchi) desu.
It's toward you.
Achira (atchi) desu.
It's over that way.

The new words in Sentence Pattern 7 are adverbial in English, but in Japanese they can be used as nouns or adverbs. Note the relationship of the following word groups: *kore, kono, koko, kochira (kotchi); sore, sono, soko, sochira (sotchi); are, ano, asoko, achira (atchi)*. Pay particular attention to the variety of meanings given to words in the *sore* group throughout the translations in this book. The words *kotchi, sotchi,* and *atchi* are more informal than *kochira, sochira,* and *achira*.

PRACTICE

1. In a hotel

(Chotto sumimasen ga) O-tearai wa doko desu ka?
 Bā
 Bābā shoppu
 Shokudō
 Kōshū denwa

(Excuse me, but) Where is the toilet?
 bar?
 barber shop?
 dining room?
 public telephone?

Practice giving answers to the above questions using:

Koko desu.	It's here.
Soko desu.	It's there.
Asoko desu.	It's over there.

2. In Tōkyō

(Chotto sumimasen ga)

 Amerika Taishikan wa dochira desu ka?
 Ginkō
 Basu no noriba
 Kusuriya
 Byōin

(Excuse me, but)

Which way is the American Embassy?
 bank?
 bus stop?
 drug store?
 hospital?

Practice answers to the above questions using:

Kochira desu.	It's this way.
Sochira desu.	It's that way (toward listener).
Achira desu.	It's over that way.

3. At the train station

Practice the following short dialogues.

Chotto sumimasen ga nimotsu ichiji azukarijo wa doko desu ka?	Excuse me, but where is the baggage check room?
Asoko desu.	It's over there.
Chotto sumimasen ga annaijo wa doko desu ka?	Excuse me, but where is the information desk?
Soko desu.	It's there.
Chotto sumimasen ga eki no baiten wa dochira desu ka?	Excuse me, but where is the station store?
Achira desu.	It's over that way.
Chotto sumimasen ga kippu uriba wa dochira desu ka?	Excuse me, but which way is the ticket counter?
Sochira desu.	It's there, in your direction.
Chotto sumimasen ga takushii noriba wa dochira desu ka?	Excuse me, but which way is the taxi stand?
Kochira desu.	It's this way.

4. Translation exercise

   (a) Excuse me, but which way is the movie theater?
   (b) Excuse me, but where is the police substation?
   (c) Excuse me, but which way is the post office?
   (d) Excuse me, but where is the train station?
   (e) Excuse me, but which way is Tōkyō Station?
   (f) Excuse me, but which way is the subway station?
   (g) Excuse me, but where is the taxi stand?
   (h) Excuse me, but where is the beauty salon?

ANSWERS: (a) *Chotto sumimasen ga eigakan wa dochira desu ka?*
(b) *Chotto sumimasen ga kōban wa doko desu ka?* (c) *Chotto sumimasen ga yūbinkyoku wa dochira desu ka?* (d) *Chotto sumimasen ga eki wa doko desu ka?* (e) *Chotto sumimasen ga Tōkyō Eki wa dochira desu ka?* (f) *Chotto sumimasen ga chikatetsu no eki wa dochira desu ka?* (g) *Chotto sumimasen ga takushii noriba wa doko desu ka?* (h) *Chotto sumimasen ga biyōin wa doko desu ka?*

◉ Situation 2: Asking what it is when you don't know

VOCABULARY

Ashino-ko	Lake Ashino
Biwa-ko	Lake Biwa
Fuji-san	Mt. Fuji
Ise Jingū	Grand Shrine of Ise
Kokkai Gijidō	National Diet Building
Kyōto Daigaku (Kyōdai)	Kyōto University
Kyūjō	Imperial Palace
Nihon-kai	Japan Sea
Nijō-jō	Nijō Castle
Ōsaka-jō	Ōsaka Castle
Ryōan-ji	Ryōan Temple
Setonai-kai	Inland Sea
Sumiyoshi Jinja	Sumiyoshi Shrine
Tōkyō Daigaku (Tōdai)	Tōkyō University

Vocabulary Note: The suffix *-dai* is short for *daigaku,* which means "university." The *Kyō-* in *Kyōdai* and the *Tō-* in *Tōdai* are contracted forms of Kyōto and Tōkyō, respectively. *Jingū* means "grand shrine," and *jinja* means "shrine." Other suffixes used in the vocabulary list are as follows:

-ji	temple	**-ko**	lake
-jō	castle	**-san**	mountain
-kai	sea		

If you're interested in architecture, handicrafts, or just identifying the things around you, the next two sentence patterns will help you get the answers that will satisfy your curiosity.

Notice again that Japanese normally makes no distinction between singular and plural. In the sentence patterns below, the words *kore, sore,* and *are* can be referring to one object, to a group of similar objects, or to a group of different objects. The context should make the intended meaning clear. In these patterns, *desu* functions like "is" or "are" in English.

Sentence Pattern 8

Kore wa / nan desu ka?	What is this?
Sore wa	What is it?
Are wa	What is that?

Sentence Pattern 9

Kore wa / NOUN desu.	This is (These are) NOUN.
Sore wa	It is (They are) NOUN.
Are wa	That is (Those are) NOUN.

Kore wa Kyōto Daigaku desu.
This is Kyōto University.
Sore wa Setonai-kai desu.
That (what you are referring to) is the Inland Sea.
Are wa Fuji-san desu.
That (over there) is Mt. Fuji.

In Lesson 2 you learned the word *nani* for "what." *Nan* is used instead of *nani* before a word beginning with *d*. Either *nan* or *nani* can be used before a word beginning with *t* or *n*. Before other consonants or vowels, only *nani* is used.

> **Kore wa nan desu ka?**
> **Nan to nani ga tabetai desu ka?**
> **Nani to nani ga tabetai desu ka?**

PRACTICE

1. On a street
   (a) Pointing to a giant paper carp flying from a pole next to a house:

Are wa nan desu ka?	What is that?
Are wa koinobori desu.	That's a *koinobori*.

   (b) Pointing to a shrine:

Are wa nan desu ka?	What is that?
Are wa jinja desu.	That's a shrine.

   (c) Looking at the small strips of paper tied onto a tree near the shrine:

Are wa nan desu ka?	What are those?
Are wa o-mikuji desu.	Those are *o-mikuji*.

   (d) Pointing to a large cluster of buildings:

Are wa nan desu ka?	What is that place over there?
Are wa Tōdai desu.	That's Tōkyō University.

Vocabulary Note: Koinobori are giant paper or cloth carp flown from poles next to houses during the celebration of Boys' Day, now called Children's Day (May 5). The carp is a symbol of strength and perseverance, hoped-for characteristics of boys.

O-mikuji are written paper fortunes that you can select after paying a small amount of money at a temple or a shrine. After reading your fortune, you fold it and attach it to a branch of a tree to bring good luck. Shrines, by the way, are Shintō and temples are Buddhist. Most Japanese belong to both.

2. In a restaurant
   (a) Pointing to the white cubes in your soup:

Kore wa nan desu ka?	What are these?
Sore wa o-tōfu desu.	That's *tōfu*.

(b) Pointing to an item on the counter of a *sushi* shop:
    Kore wa nan desu ka?   What is this?
    Kore wa uni desu.   This is sea urchin.

(c) Pointing to your friend's drink:
    Sore wa nan desu ka?   What is that?
    Kore wa remonēdo desu.   This is lemonade.

(d) Pointing to what is being served at another table:
    Are wa nan desu ka?   What's that over there?
    Are wa unagi teishoku desu.   That's the full-course eel dinner.

◈ **Situation 3: Finding out what it is (and isn't)**

Look again at Sentence Patterns 8 and 9 and compare them with the two below.

Sentence Pattern 8A

Kore wa / NOUN desu ka?   Is this NOUN?
Sore wa   it
Are wa   that

Kore wa Shinjuku Eki desu ka?
Is this Shinjuku Station?
Sore wa hanga desu ka?
Are they (what you have) woodblock prints?
Are wa yūbinkyoku desu ka?
Is that a post office?

To express the negative, use *ja arimasen* (a bit informal) or *de wa arimasen* (more polite) after the noun. Compare:
    Kore wa yūbinkyoku desu.
    Kore wa yūbinkyoku ja arimasen.
                    de wa arimasen.

─────── **Sentence Pattern 10** ───────

Kore wa / NOUN ja arimasen.　　This isn't NOUN.
　　　　　　　de wa arimasen.
Sore wa　　　　　　　　　　　It
Are wa　　　　　　　　　　　　That

───────────────

Kore wa yūbinkyoku ja arimasen.
This isn't a post office.
Sore wa ginkō ja arimasen.
It isn't a bank.
Are wa Tanaka-san ja arimasen.
That isn't Mr. Tanaka.

Review the expansion of some of the patterns you have learned in this lesson.

S.P. 8: **Kore wa nan desu ka?**
S.P. 9: **Kore wa yūbinkyoku desu.**
S.P. 8A: **Kore wa yūbinkyoku desu ka?**
S.P. 10: **Kore wa yūbinkyoku ja arimasen.**

The affirmative *Kore wa yūbinkyoku desu* and the negative *Kore wa yūbinkyoku ja arimasen* can be used to respond to the question *Kore wa yūbinkyoku desu ka?* by using the word *hai* (*ē*) or *iie* that you have already learned. Recall:

Unagi ga tabetai desu ka?
Hai, tabetai desu. [*or*]
Iie, tabetaku arimasen.

Now, using the patterns in this lesson:

Kore wa yūbinkyoku desu ka?
Hai, (kore wa) yūbinkyoku desu. [*or*]
Iie, (kore wa) yūbinkyoku ja arimasen.

The topic *kore wa* is optional in the answer since it is usually understood from the context of the situation.

PRACTICE

Give affirmative and negative responses to each of the following questions.

1. **Kore wa yūbinkyoku desu ka?**   Is this a post office?
2. **Are wa unagi desu ka?**   Are those eels?
3. **Sore wa o-tōfu desu ka?**   Is that (which you are eating) *tōfu?*
4. **Are wa jinja desu ka?**   Is that a shrine?
5. **Kore wa Shinjuku Eki desu ka?**   Is this Shinjuku Station?
6. **Are wa Tōdai desu ka?**   Is that Tōkyō University?
7. **Kore wa basu no noriba desu ka?**   Is this the bus stop?

ANSWERS: 1. *Hai, (kore wa) yūbinkyoku desu. Iie, (kore wa) yūbinkyoku ja arimasen.* 2. *Hai, (are wa) unagi desu. Iie, (are wa) unagi ja arimasen.* 3. *Hai, (kore wa) o-tōfu desu. Iie, (kore wa) o-tōfu ja arimasen.* 4. *Hai, (are wa) jinja desu. Iie, (are wa) jinja ja arimasen.* 5. *Hai, (kore wa) Shinjuku Eki desu. Iie, (kore wa) Shinjuku Eki ja arimasen.* 6. *Hai, (are wa) Tōdai desu. Iie, (are wa) Tōdai ja arimasen.* 7. *Hai, (kore wa) basu no noriba desu. Iie, (kore wa) basu no noriba ja arimasen.*

When asked a question like "Is this the post office?" however, it is usually unnecessary to repeat the noun in question when answering, just as in English when we say "Yes, it is" or "No, it isn't." The following sentence patterns show the comparable short responses in Japanese.

─────── **Sentence Pattern 11** ───────

Hai (Ē) / sō desu.   Yes, it is (they are).

Sentence Pattern 12

Iie / sō ja arimasen.   No, it isn't (they aren't).
       de wa arimasen.

Kore wa ginkō desu ka?
Is this a bank?
Hai, sō desu.
Yes, it is.
Iie, sō ja arimasen.
No, it isn't.

Are wa unagi desu ka?
Is that eel?
Hai, sō desu.
Yes, it is.
Iie, sō ja arimasen.
No, it isn't.

PRACTICE

Use these two short responses to give affirmative and negative answers to the practice questions on page 64.

◈ **Situation 4: Asking about the family**

VOCABULARY

Kinship Terms:

For you	For others	
chichi	o-tō-san	father
haha	o-kā-san	mother
kodomo	o-ko-san	child
musuko	musuko-san	son
musume	musume-san (o-jō-san)	daughter
kanai	oku-san	wife
shujin	go-shujin	husband

Personal Pronouns:

anata	you
kare	he
kanojo	she
watakushi	I

Nationalities:

Amerikajin	American (person)
Furansujin	French
Hawaijin	Hawaiian
Igirisujin	English
Itariajin	Italian
Kanadajin	Canadian
Nihonjin	Japanese
Ōsutorariajin	Australian
Supeinjin	Spanish

Occupations:

bijinesuman	businessman
eki-in	station employee
gakusei	student
ginkōin	bank employee
haisha	dentist
hisho	secretary
hosutesu	hostess (in a bar or cabaret)
isha (o-isha-san)	medical doctor
kangofu	nurse
keikan (o-mawari-san)	policeman
kōkanshu (denwa no kōkanshu)	telephone operator
sarariiman	white-collar employee
sensei	teacher
shachō	company president
shashō	train or bus conductor
ten-in	store clerk
untenshu	driver

Vocabulary Note: In the above list kinship terms are divided into two groups. The first group is used when you refer to those in your own family. The next group shows terms of respect used when you refer to or ask about those in another person's family. The Japanese are very observant of this distinction. When addressing his own father or mother, however, a Japanese will use *o-tō-san* or *o-kā-san* to show respect. When directly addressing his son or daughter, a Japanese will usually use the personal name rather than the kinship term. A more complete list of these kinship terms appears in the Appendix.

Japanese also have several other words for "I" and "you," but since their correct usage requires considerable familiarity with Japanese social structure, you are advised to stick to *watakushi* for yourself and *anata* (or, preferably, the family name with the suffix *-san*) for the person with whom you are speaking. The following alternate forms are provided, since you will probably hear them often.

boku	I—male speaker, informal
ore	I—male speaker, very informal
watashi	I—a bit more informal than *watakushi*
kimi	you—male speaker, informal
o-mae	you—for children and inferiors
o-taku	you—polite

The Japanese are much more comfortable using the family name + *-san* than they are using such words as *kare, kanojo,* and *anata.* The suffix *-san* can mean "Mr.," "Mrs.," "Miss," or "Ms.," but you needn't think of it as stuffy or too formal. The suffix *-chan* is attached to children's first names: *Kazuko-chan, Mieko-chan, Ken-chan,* etc. When addressing or referring to teachers or doctors, the word *sensei* is used after the family name: *Satō Sensei, Yamamoto Sensei,* etc.

O-isha-san and *o-mawari-san* can be used to address doctors and policemen instead of the name plus *sensei* or *-san.* NEVER use *-san* with your own name.

Use the following sentence pattern to find out more about the people with whom you are speaking and their families.

Sentence Pattern 8B

PERSON wa / NOUN desu ka?   Is PERSON a NOUN?
PERSON no PERSON wa /   Is PERSON (of PERSON)
  NOUN desu ka?   a NOUN?

Tanaka-san wa Nihonjin desu ka?
Is Mr. (Mrs., etc.) Tanaka Japanese?
Oku-san wa hisho desu ka?
Is your wife a secretary?
Tanaka-san no o-tō-san wa sarariiman desu ka?
Is Mr. Tanaka's father a white-collar employee?
O-tō-san no oku-san wa Amerikajin desu ka?
Is your father's wife an American?

Sentence Pattern 8B is merely an expansion of the patterns you have learned in this lesson. An important addition, though, is the particle *no* to indicate that the following noun "belongs" to the preceding one. Thus, *Tanaka-san no o-tō-san* means "Mr. Tanaka's father," and *Otō-san no oku-san* means "your father's wife." Notice that because Japanese has two distinct vocabularies for family relationships, *anata no* in a phrase like *anata no oku-san* (your wife) would be redundant.

When answering a question like *Tanaka-san wa Nihonjin desu ka?* the affirmative short response, *Hai, sō desu,* is perfectly appropriate. The negative short response, *Iie, sō ja arimasen,* is also correct, but usually you want to give a bit more information to clarify your answer.

Tanaka-san wa Nihonjin desu ka?

Hai, (Tanaka-san wa) Nihonjin desu. [*or*]
Hai, sō desu. [*but*]
Iie, (Tanaka-san wa) Nihonjin ja arimasen.
   Amerikajin desu. [*or*]
Iie, sō ja arimasen. Amerikajin desu.

Mr. Tanaka is not a Japanese. He's an American.

Oku-san wa hisho desu ka?
   Hai, sō desu. [*but*]
Iie, (kanai wa) hisho ja arimasen. Ten-in desu. [*or*]
Iie, sō ja arimasen. Ten-in desu. [*or*]
Iie, ten-in desu.

My wife (is not a secretary. She) is a clerk.

PRACTICE

1. Answer in the affirmative.

Anata wa Amerikajin desu ka?	Are you an American?
Hai, sō desu.	Yes, I am.
O-ko-san wa gakusei desu ka?	Is your son (*or* daughter) a student?
Hai, sō desu.	Yes, he (*or* she) is.
Musume-san wa ginkōin desu ka?	Is your daughter a bank employee?
Hai, sō desu.	Yes, she is.

2. Answer in the negative.

Anata wa sensei desu ka?	Are you a teacher?
Iie. (Sensei ja arimasen.) **Gakusei desu.**	No. (I'm not a teacher.) I'm a student.
Tanaka-san wa keikan desu ka?	Is Mr. Tanaka a policeman?
Iie. (Keikan ja arimasen.) Unten-shu desu.	No. (He is not a policeman.) He's a driver.

Oku-san wa hisho desu ka? — Is your wife a secretary?
Iie. (Hisho ja arimasen.) Ten-in desu. — No. (She is not a secretary.) She's a clerk.

3. Answer in the negative.

Tanaka-san no o-tō-san wa haisha desu ka? — Is Mr. Tanaka's father a dentist?
Iie, (Tanaka-san no o-tō-san wa) sensei desu. — No, (Mr. Tanaka's father is) a teacher.

Musuko-san wa gakusei desu ka? — Is your son a student?
Iie, (musuko wa) sarariiman desu. — No, (my son is) a white-collar employee.

~~~~~~ Sentence Patterns Covered in This Lesson ~~~~~~

6. (Chotto sumimasen ga) / PLACE wa / doko desu ka?
   (Chotto sumimasen ga) / PLACE wa / dochira desu ka?
7. NOUN OF DIRECTION desu.
8. Kore wa / nan desu ka?
   Sore wa
   Are wa
8A. Kore wa / NOUN desu ka?
   Sore wa
   Are wa
8B. PERSON wa / NOUN desu ka?
   PERSON no PERSON wa / NOUN desu ka?
9. Kore wa / NOUN desu.
   Sore wa
   Are wa
10. Kore wa / NOUN ja arimasen.
                de wa arimasen.
   Sore wa
   Are wa
11. Hai (Ē) / sō desu.
12. Iie / sō ja arimasen.
            de wa arimasen.

LESSON 4

Now that you have learned how to get your bearings and how to express your needs in Japanese, it's time to begin thinking of "we" as well as "I." After all, so many things are more fun when the experience is shared. In this lesson you will learn to make suggestions to and ask advice from your Japanese friends about the things you can do together —trips, sports, shopping, eating, enjoying.

◀ Situation 1: Making suggestions

VOCABULARY

shimashō	Let's do (it).

Sports and Games:

bōringu	bowling
dansu	dancing
gorufu	golf
sukēto	skating
sukii	skiing
tenisu	tennis

Others:

benkyō	study
kekkon	marriage
kembutsu	sightseeing

renshū	practice
ryokō	travel, trip
sampo	a walk
shokuji	meal

Sentence Pattern 13

VERB-INFINITIVE + -mashō.   Let's VERB.

Iki- + -mashō   Ikimashō.
Let's go.
Kai- + -mashō   Kaimashō.
Let's buy.
Mi- + -mashō   Mimashō.
Let's see. (Let's watch.)
Nomi- + -mashō   Nomimashō.
Let's drink.
Shi- + -mashō   Shimashō.
Let's do (it).
Tabe- + -mashō   Tabemashō.
Let's eat.

The sentence pattern VERB-INFINITIVE + *-mashō* is used to propose an action to somebody else. Compare this with the pattern you learned in Lesson 2 that meant "I would like to VERB": VERB-INFINITIVE + *-tai desu*. Note that even in the absence of a subject or object, both are complete sentences.

Ikitai desu.	Ikimashō.
Kaitai desu.	Kaimashō.
Mitai desu.	Mimashō.
Nomitai desu.	Nomimashō.
Tabetai desu.	Tabemashō.
Shitai desu.	Shimashō.

The following two sentence patterns are Sentence Pattern 13 plus a noun that shows what it is you are suggesting.

——————————— Sentence Pattern 14 ———————————

NOUN O / VERB-INFINITIVE   Let's VERB NOUN.
   + -mashō.

Sukiyaki o tabemashō.
Let's eat *sukiyaki.*
O-sake o nomimashō.
Let's drink sakè.
Kabuki o mimashō.
Let's see a Kabuki play.
Gorufu o shimashō.
Let's play golf.
Kimono o kaimashō.
Let's buy a kimono.

——————————— Sentence Pattern 15 ———————————

PLACE e / ikimashō.   Let's go to PLACE.

Yokohama e ikimashō.
Let's go to Yokohama.
Eiga e ikimashō.
Let's go to a movie.
O-sushiya e ikimashō.
Let's go to a *sushi* shop.

The particle *o* in this pattern is the same *o* that was used in Lesson 1—*Biiru o kudasai.* That is, it shows the object of the verb—what you would like to do, eat, drink, etc. Compare the following:

Sukiyaki ga tabetai desu.	**Sukiyaki o tabemashō.**
Kimono ga kaitai desu.	**Kimono o kaimashō.**
O-sake ga nomitai desu.	**O-sake o nomimashō.**

Shimashō comes from the verb *suru* (this verb form will be explained later), which generally means "to do." It is the most frequently used Japanese verb because of its ability to allow an object-noun to function somewhat like a verb, much as "I do writing" might be equivalent to "I write" in English. Because many of the object-nouns used with *suru* were originally Chinese words, *suru* is often called the "Chinese" verb. But since *suru* has now come to be used with many English and other foreign-language nouns as well, perhaps a better name for it would be the "foreign" verb. The following are examples of nouns from English that are used with *suru* to express action.

Gorufu o shimashō.	Let's play golf.
Tenisu o shimashō.	Let's play tennis.
Dansu o shimashō.	Let's dance.
Bōringu o shimashō.	Let's bowl.
Sukii o shimashō.	Let's ski.

PRACTICE

1. At a restaurant

Sukiyaki o tabemashō. **Tempura** **O-sushi** **Tonkatsu** **Bifuteki**	Let's eat *sukiyaki.* *tempura.* *sushi.* pork cutlets. beefsteak.

2. At a coffee shop

Kōhii o nomimashō. **O-kōcha**	Let's have (drink) coffee. English tea.

{ Kēki o tabemashō. { Aisukuriimu	Let's have (eat) { cake. { ice cream.

3. At a bar

{ Biiru o nomimashō. { O-sake	Let's have (drink) { beer. { sakè.

4. At a department store

{ Kamera o kaimashō. { Kono kamera { Sono rajio	Let's buy { a camera. { this camera. { that radio.

5. On dates or other social occasions

{ Gorufu o shimashō. { Tenisu { Bōringu { Dansu	Let's { play golf. { play tennis. { go bowling. { dance.
{ Ano eiga o mimashō. { Ano Kabuki { Ano Bunraku { Kono eiga	Let's see { that movie. { that Kabuki play. { that puppet play. { this movie.
{ Nara e ikimashō. { Ōsaka { Kyōto { Hiroshima	Let's go to { Nara. { Ōsaka. { Kyōto. { Hiroshima.

◈ Situation 2: Asking for suggestions

Sentence Pattern 14A

NOUN O / VERB-INFINITIVE   Shall we VERB NOUN?
  + -mashō ka?

Sukiyaki o tabemashō ka?	Shall we eat *sukiyaki?*
Biiru o nomimashō ka?	Shall we drink beer?
Kabuki o mimashō ka?	Shall we see a Kabuki play?
Kimono o kaimashō ka?	Shall we buy a kimono?
Tenisu o shimashō ka?	Shall we play tennis?

Sentence Pattern 15A

PLACE, NOUN e / iki-   Shall we go to PLACE,
   mashō ka?   NOUN?

Nihon e ikimashō ka?   Shall we go to Japan?
Eiga e ikimashō ka?   Shall we go to a movie?

Compare *Biiru o nomimashō* and *Biiru o nomimashō ka?*
In both cases you are making a suggestion to someone
else, but the question form is less abrupt because it asks
directly for the other person's agreement. Since this latter
type of suggestion is expressed as a question, you usually
answer in the following way:

Ē, tabemashō.   Yes, let's eat (it, some).
Ē, nomimashō.   Yes, let's drink (it, some).

The following sentence patterns are very useful when you
want to go somewhere or do something but don't know
what to suggest.

Sentence Pattern 14B

Nani o / VERB-INFINITIVE   What shall we VERB?
  + -mashō ka?
Dore o / VERB-INFINITIVE   Which one shall we
  + -mashō ka?   VERB?

Nani o (Dore o) tabemashō ka?
What (Which one) shall we eat?
Nani o (Dore o) nomimashō ka?
What (Which one) shall we drink?
Nani o (Dore o) shimashō ka?
What (Which one) shall we do?

—————— **Sentence Pattern 15B** ——————

Doko e / ikimashō ka?   Where shall we go?

PRACTICE

1. Practice the following short dialogues.

Nani o tabemashō ka?	What shall we eat?
Bifuteki o tabemashō.	Let's have steak.
Nani o nomimashō ka?	What shall we drink?
O-sake o nomimashō.	Let's drink sakè.
Nani o shimashō ka?	What shall we do?
Tenisu o shimashō.	Let's play tennis.
Doko e ikimashō ka?	Where shall we go?
Kyōto e ikimashō.	Let's go to Kyōto.
Nani o kaimashō ka?	What shall we buy?
Kamera o kaimashō.	Let's buy a camera.
Nani o mimashō ka?	What shall we see?
Ano eiga o mimashō.	Let's see that movie.

2. Translate into Japanese:

   (a) Let's bowl.
   (b) Let's study.
   (c) Let's go to Kyōto.
   (d) Let's take a walk.
   (e) Let's play tennis.
   (f) Let's play golf.
   (g) Let's practice.
   (h) Let's go to Mt. Fuji.
   (i) Let's eat *sukiyaki.*
   (j) Let's buy this camera.
   (k) Let's go to that movie.
   (l) Let's drink sakè.
   (m) Let's go to that photo studio.
   (n) Let's go to the train station.
   (o) Let's see this Kabuki play.
   (p) Let's drink tea.

ANSWERS: (a) *Bōringu o shimashō.* (b) *Benkyō o shimashō.* (c) *Kyōto e ikimashō.* (d) *Sampo o shimashō.* (e) *Tenisu o shimashō.* (f) *Gorufu o shimashō.* (g) *Renshū o shimashō.* (h) *Fuji-san e ikimashō.* (i) *Sukiyaki o tabemashō.* (j) *Kono kamera o kaimashō.* (k) *Ano eiga e ikimashō.* (l) *O-sake o nomimashō.* (m) *Ano shashin-ya e ikimashō.* (n) *Eki e ikimashō.* (o) *Kono Kabuki o mimashō.* (p) *O-cha o nomimashō.*

3. Practice the following short dialogues.

Dore o kaimashō ka?	Which one shall we buy?
Kono kamera o kaimashō ka?	Shall we buy this camera?
Ē, kaimashō.	Yes, let's buy it.
Doko e ikimashō ka?	Where shall we go?
Kyōto e ikimashō ka?	Shall we go to Kyōto?
Kyōto e ikitai desu ka?	Would you like to go to Kyōto?
Hai, ikitai desu.	Yes, I'd like to.
Ano eiga ga mitai desu ka?	Would you like to see that movie?
Iie. Mitaku arimasen.	No, I wouldn't.
Doko e ikimashō ka?	Where shall we go?
Kabuki e ikimashō ka?	Shall we go to Kabuki?
Ē, ikimashō.	Yes, let's go.
Are wa nan desu ka?	What's that?
Are wa jinja desu. Mitai desu ka?	That's a shrine. Would you like to see it?
Hai. Mitai desu. Ikimashō ka?	Yes, I would. Shall we go?
Ē, ikimashō.	Yes, let's go.
Kore wa nan desu ka?	What is this?
Sore wa unagi desu. Tabetai desu ka?	That's eel. Would you like to eat some?
Iie, tabetaku arimasen.	No, I wouldn't.
Nani ga tabetai desu ka?	What would you like to eat?
Kore to kore wa nan desu ka?	What are these things here?
Sore wa teishoku desu. Tabemashō ka?	That's the full-course dinner. Shall we have that?
Ē, tabemashō.	Yes, let's.

OTHER USEFUL VERBS

Some useful new verbs and examples of the particles used with them are listed below in sentence form. Dropping the *-mashō* at the end of each verb will give you the verb-infinitive, to which you can add the *-tai desu* ending that you have already studied or other verb endings that will be presented later. Alternative particles are given in parentheses.

NOUN o agemashō.	Let's give NOUN.
PERSON ni (to) aimashō.	Let's meet SOMEONE.
NOUN o araimashō.	Let's wash NOUN.
Arukimashō.	Let's walk.
NOUN o dashimashō.	Let's mail NOUN.
Dekakemashō.	Let's go out.
Demashō.	Let's leave (this place).
PLACE e (ni) hairimashō.	Let's enter PLACE.
NOUN o hajimemashō.	Let's begin NOUN.
Hanashimashō.	Let's talk.
O-kane o haraimashō.	Let's pay the money.
Iimashō.	Let's say (this).
Isogimashō.	Let's hurry.
Kaerimashō.	Let's return home.
NOUN o kaeshimashō.	Let's return NOUN.
Denwa o kakemashō.	Let's make a telephone call.
NOUN o kakimashō.	Let's write NOUN.
Kangaemashō.	Let's think (about that).
NOUN o karimashō.	Let's borrow NOUN.
NOUN o kashimashō.	Let's lend NOUN.
Kikimashō.	Let's listen (*or* inquire).
Kimemashō.	Let's decide on this.
PERSON o machimashō.	Let's wait for PERSON.
PLACE de machimashō.	Let's wait at PLACE.
Hidari e (ni) magarimashō.	Let's turn to the left.

Migi e (ni) magarimashō.	Let's turn to the right.
Koko o magarimashō.	Let's turn here.
NOUN **o naraimashō.**	Let's learn NOUN.
Nemashō.	Let's go to sleep.
Norikaemashō.	Let's change (trains).
VEHICLE **ni norimashō.**	Let's get in (on) VEHICLE.
NOUN **o okurimashō.**	Let's send NOUN.
VEHICLE **kara (o) orimashō.**	Let's get off VEHICLE.
PLACE **de orimashō.**	Let's get off at PLACE.
PLACE **ni suwarimashō.**	Let's sit at PLACE.
NOUN **o tsukurimashō.**	Let's make NOUN.
NOUN **o yamemashō.**	Let's stop NOUN.
Yasumimashō.	Let's rest.
Gakkō o yasumimashō.	Let's cut class.
Kaisha o yasumimashō.	Let's not go to work.
PERSON **o yobimashō.**	Let's call PERSON.
NOUN **o yomimashō.**	Let's read NOUN.

~~~~~~~ **Sentence Patterns Covered in This Lesson** ~~~~~~~

13. VERB-INFINITIVE + -mashō.
14. NOUN o / VERB-INFINITIVE + -mashō.
14A. NOUN o / VERB-INFINITIVE + -mashō ka?
14B. Nani o / VERB-INFINITIVE + -mashō ka?
     Dore o VERB-INFINITIVE + -mashō ka?
15. PLACE e / ikimashō.
15A. PLACE, NOUN e / ikimashō ka?
15B. Doko e / ikimashō ka?

LESSON 5

If you go to a restaurant or scenic place in Japan, you will want to be able to show your appreciation to your host by commenting on how good the food is or how beautiful the view. If you are traveling around Japan by yourself, you will want to be able to tell the innkeeper or the waiter what your preferences are. The adjectives and descriptive nouns presented in this lesson will help you do just that.

◈ Situation 1: Describing things

VOCABULARY

Adjectives:

atarashii	new; fresh
furui	old; used (for things)
hayai	fast; early
osoi	slow; late
hiroi	spacious; wide
semai	cramped; narrow
ii	good
warui	bad
katai	hard, tough (texture)
yawarakai	soft, tender (texture)

nagai	long
mijikai	short
ōi	plentiful; large in portion
sukunai	scarce; skimpy in portion
ōkii	big, large
chiisai	small
takai	expensive; high
hikui	low
yasui	inexpensive, cheap
tōi	far
chikai	near
wakai	young
atatakai (attakai)	warm (weather, objects, persons)
suzushii	cool (weather)
mushiatsui	muggy, hot and humid
atsui	hot (weather, objects)
samui	cold (weather)
tsumetai	cold (objects)
amai	sweet tasting
karai	salty; soy-saucy; spicy
nigai	bitter
suppai	sour
oishii	tasty; delicious
mazui	not tasty; unappetizing
omoshiroi	interesting; entertaining; funny
tanoshii	enjoyable
tsumaranai	uninteresting; boring; not enjoyable
yasashii	easy, simple; tender (person)
muzukashii	difficult; fussy (person)

isogashii	busy
kanashii	sad
sabishii	lonely
ureshii	glad
uttōshii	depressing; oppressive

Nouns:

densha	electric train
Eigo	the English language
hi	day
hito	person
Nihongo	the Japanese language
o-ryōri	cooking; cuisine
o-tenki	the weather
piano	piano
Shinkansen	high-speed bullet train
uchi (ie)	home (house)

Adverbs of Time:

ashita	tomorrow
kinō	yesterday
kyō	today
kesa	this morning
komban	this evening
konogoro	these days

Vocabulary Note: In English, "old" is used to describe both people and things. In Japanese, however, the adjective *furui* applies only to things. Although *wakai* is used to describe an individual who is young, there is no Japanese adjective meaning "old" to characterize people. Instead, Japanese people use the noun *toshiyori* to designate an elderly person.

The word "cold" is used in English to describe both weather and the temperature of objects. In Japanese, *samui* is used for cold weather, and *tsumetai* is used for objects cold to the touch. *Atsui* is not used for "hot" with the word for "water." Instead, the noun *o-yu* is used for hot or boiling water.

Yasashii, which can mean "tender" when referring to the character of a person, never refers to food in Japanese. For tender meat or items having a soft texture, *yawarakai* is used. Hardness or toughness is expressed by *katai.*

The word *uchi* is often used to mean "household" or "family." It can also be used like the word "house" in English, but normally *ie* is used to designate "house."

Sentence Pattern 16

ADJECTIVE desu.   It is ADJECTIVE.

Atarashii desu.
It's new.
Nagai desu.
It's long.
Takai desu.
It's expensive.
Atsui desu.
It's hot.
Oishii desu.
It's delicious.
Omoshiroi desu.
It's interesting.
Muzukashii desu.
It's difficult.

Remember that *desu* was used in Lesson 2 to make the sentence *Tabetai desu* more polite. Similarly, to say *Takai* rather than *Takai desu* means the same thing but is considered informal.

You will often hear Japanese use the exclamatory word *nē* at the end of a sentence or phrase, particularly when that sentence or phrase contains an adjective.

Takai desu nē.

The *nē* in *Takai desu nē* invites the listener's agreement. It is similar to the English "isn't it?" but is used much more often.

PRACTICE

Practice the following short sentences.

Takai desu nē.	It's expensive, isn't it?
Yasui desu nē.	It's cheap, isn't it?
Ōkii desu nē.	It's big, isn't it?
Chiisai desu nē.	It's small, isn't it?
Nagai desu nē.	It's long, isn't it?
Mijikai desu nē.	It's short, isn't it?
Ii desu nē.	It's good, isn't it?
Warui desu nē.	It's bad, isn't it?
Tōi desu nē.	It's far, isn't it?
Chikai desu nē.	It's near, isn't it?
Hayai desu nē.	It's fast, isn't it? [*or*] It's early, isn't it?
Osoi desu nē.	It's slow, isn't it? [*or*] It's late, isn't it?

THE CONJUGATION OF ADJECTIVES

Unlike English adjectives, Japanese adjectives take new forms to denote past and negative usages. As you may have already noticed, Japanese adjectives all end in *-i*. What precedes this *-i* is called the adjective stem, to which past and negative endings are added.

THE POLITE PAST AFFIRMATIVE

You form the polite past tense of adjectives by adding *-katta desu* to the adjective stem.

polite present	Ōkii desu.	It is big.
adjective stem	ōki-	
polite past	Ōkikatta desu.	It was big.
	Osokatta desu.	It was slow. [*or*] It was late.

The *desu* here only serves to make the adjective polite. *Ōkikatta* by itself is past tense and informal.

THE POLITE PRESENT NEGATIVE

You form the polite negative of adjectives by adding *-ku arimasen* to the adjective stem.

polite present	Ōkii desu.	It is big.
adjective stem	ōki-	
polite pres./neg.	Ōkiku arimasen.	It is not big.
	Osoku arimasen.	It is not slow. [*or*] It is not late.

Summary of Adjective Conjugation

Adj. (informal)	Meaning	Adjective Stem	Present
ōkii	big	ōki-	Ōkii desu.
atarashii	new	atarashi-	Atarashii desu.
hayai	fast; early	haya-	Hayai desu.
ii	good	yo-	Ii desu.
warui	bad	waru-	Warui desu.
oishii	delicious	oishi-	Oishii desu.
takai	expensive	taka-	Takai desu.
yasui	cheap	yasu-	Yasui desu.
omoshiroi	interesting	omoshiro-	Omoshiroi desu.

THE POLITE PAST NEGATIVE

You form the polite past negative of adjectives by adding *deshita* to the polite present negative.

polite present	**Ōkii desu.**	It is big.
adjective stem	**ōki-**	
polite pres./neg.	**Ōkiku arimasen.**	It is not big.
polite past./neg.	**Ōkiku arimasen deshita.**	It was not big.
	Chiisaku arimasen deshita.	It was not small.
	Osoku arimasen deshita.	It was not slow. [*or*] It was not late.

Deshita (as in *Ōkiku arimasen deshita*) is the past tense of *desu*.

Ii, "good," is the only adjective whose stem is irregular.

(Polite Forms)

Past	Present Negative	Past Negative
Ōkikatta desu.	Ōkiku arimasen.	Ōkiku arimasen deshita.
Atarashikatta desu.	Atarashiku arimasen.	Atarashiku arimasen deshita.
Hayakatta desu.	Hayaku arimasen.	Hayaku arimasen deshita.
Yokatta desu.	Yoku arimasen.	Yoku arimasen deshita.
Warukatta desu.	Waruku arimasen.	Waruku arimasen deshita.
Oishikatta desu.	Oishiku arimasen.	Oishiku arimasen deshita.
Takakatta desu.	Takaku arimasen.	Takaku arimasen deshita.
Yasukatta desu.	Yasuku arimasen.	Yasuku arimasen deshita.
Omoshirokatta desu.	Omoshiroku arimasen.	Omoshiroku arimasen deshita.

The adjective stem of *ii* is *yo-*, based on *yoi*, an older form of *ii*.

Ii desu.	It is good.
yo-	(adjective stem)
Yokatta desu.	It was good.
Yoku arimasen.	It is not good.
Yoku arimasen deshita.	It was not good.

PRACTICE

1. See whether you can translate the following English sentences into Japanese.

- (a) It's expensive, isn't it?
- (b) It's cheap, isn't it?
- (c) It's large, isn't it?
- (d) It's small, isn't it?
- (e) It's long, isn't it?
- (f) It's short, isn't it?

ANSWERS: (a) *Takai desu nē.* (b) *Yasui desu nē.* (c) *Ōkii desu nē.* (d) *Chiisai desu nē.* (e) *Nagai desu nē.* (f) *Mijikai desu nē.*

2. Form the polite present negative as shown in the example below.

EXAMPLE: **Takai desu.**   *Takaku arimasen.*

Yasui desu.	**Suzushii desu.**
Hiroi desu.	**Atatakai desu.**
Semai desu.	**Nagai desu.**
Atsui desu.	**Mijikai desu.**
Samui desu.	

3. Form the polite past as shown in the example below.

EXAMPLE: **Karai desu.**   *Karakatta desu.*

Amai desu.	**Chiisai desu.**
Atarashii desu.	**Ōkii desu.**
Furui desu.	**Ii desu.**
Wakai desu.	**Warui desu.**

4. Form the polite past negative as shown in the example below.

EXAMPLE: **Tōi desu.** *Tōku arimasen deshita.*

Chikai desu.	**Oishii desu.**
Omoshiroi desu.	**Mazui desu.**
Tsumaranai desu.	**Yasashii desu.**
Atsui desu.	**Muzukashii desu.**
Samui desu.	

⬧ **Situation 2: Describing things** *(continued)*

Sentence Pattern 16A

ΓOPIC wa / ADJECTIVE desu.   TOPIC is ADJECTIVE.

Kore wa takai desu.
This is expensive.
Are wa oishii desu.
That is delicious.
Sore wa atarashii desu.
It is new.
Kono kamera wa takai desu.
This camera is expensive.
Kono sūpu wa oishii desu.
This soup is delicious.

Remember that *wa* denotes the topic of the sentence—what you are talking or asking about.

This sentence pattern can also be used with the past tense of adjectives and with the present and past negative forms.

Kono kamera wa takakatta desu.	This camera was expensive.
Ano sūpu wa oishiku arimasen.	That soup does not taste good.

Sono terebi wa yoku arimasen deshita.

That television set was not good.

Now compare the following sentence pattern with Sentence Pattern 16A.

Sentence Pattern 17

ADJECTIVE NOUN desu.   It's a ADJECTIVE NOUN.

Takai terebi desu.
It's an expensive television set.
Yasui rajio desu.
It's an inexpensive radio.
Atarashii terebi desu.
It's a new television set.
Furui terebi desu.
It's an old television set.
Ii kamera desu.
It's a good camera.
Warui kamera desu.
It's a poor camera.
Omoshiroi eiga desu.
It's an interesting movie.
Tanoshii eiga desu.
It's an enjoyable movie.
Tsumaranai eiga desu.
It's a boring movie.

Now compare Sentence Patterns 16A and 17 in the polite past tense.

S.P. 16A: **Eiga wa omoshiro-katta desu.**

The movie was interesting.

S.P. 17: **Omoshiroi eiga deshita.**

It was an interesting movie.

Compare Sentence Patterns 16A and 17 in the polite present negative form.

S.P. 16A: **Eiga wa omoshi-**   The movie is not interesting.
         roku arimasen.

S.P. 17:   **Omoshiroi eiga ja**   It is not an interesting movie.
         arimasen.

Compare Sentence Patterns 16A and 17 in the polite past negative form.

S.P. 16A: **Eiga wa omoshi-**   The movie was not interesting.
         roku arimasen
         deshita.

S.P. 17:   **Omoshiroi eiga ja**   It was not an interesting movie.
         arimasen deshita.

The addition of a topic to Sentence Pattern 17 results in the following kind of sentence.

Sentence Pattern 17A

TOPIC   wa / ADJECTIVE   Topic is a ADJECTIVE
   NOUN desu.   NOUN.

Kore wa oishii tempura desu.
This is a delicious plate of *tempura*.
Are wa takai resutoran desu.
That is an expensive restaurant.
Tanaka-san wa ii sensei desu.
Mr. Tanaka is a good teacher.

Study carefully the following examples of the patterns you have learned so far in this lesson. Note their similarities and differences.

S.P. 16: **Atarashii desu.**

S.P. 16A: **Kono terebi wa / atarashii desu.**
S.P. 17: **Atarashii terebi desu.**
S.P. 17A: **Kore wa / atarashii terebi desu.**

PRACTICE

1. Practice with Sentence Pattern 16A.

(a) Use any of the following topics and adjectives to make reasonable sentences that contain polite present adjective forms.

EXAMPLE: **Kono terebi wa atarashii desu.**

Topics	Adjectives
eiga	**tsumaranai**
terebi	**atarashii**
o-sushi	**oishii**
yūbinkyoku	**takai**
Nihon	**tōi**
kamera	**semai**
kore, sore, are	**omoshiroi**
kono, sono, ano NOUN	**nagai**
	chiisai
	yasui

(b) Now use the word list in (a) to make sentences containing polite past, polite present negative, and polite past negative adjective forms.

EXAMPLES: **Sono terebi wa atarashikatta desu.**
Sono terebi wa atarashiku arimasen.
Sono terebi wa atarashiku arimasen deshita.

2. Practice with Sentence Pattern 17.

(a) Point to things in your room and describe them.
EXAMPLE: **Takai kamera desu.**

(b) Think of some things you used to own and describe them.

EXAMPLE: **Takai kamera deshita.**

3. Practice with Sentence Pattern 17A.
   (a) Point to things in your room and describe them.
       EXAMPLES: **Kore wa atarashii terebi desu.**
                 Are wa ii kamera desu.

   (b) Now describe things as they were in the past.
       EXAMPLES: **Kore wa atarashii terebi deshita.**
                 Sore wa ii kamera deshita.

   (c) Recall several movies you have seen and describe them.
   Use adjectives like *ii, warui, tsumaranai, tanoshii, atarashii,* and
   furui.

       EXAMPLES: NAME OF THE MOVIE **wa omoshiroi eiga
                 deshita.**
                 **Ano eiga wa omoshiroi eiga ja arimasen
                 deshita.**

   (d) Recall a meal you have eaten and describe it.
       EXAMPLES: **Are wa oishii tempura deshita.**
                 Are wa mazui tempura deshita.
                 Are wa takai hambāgā deshita.

◈ Situation 3: Talking about this and that

1. Talking about the weather
   The following list of words and phrases will come in
handy when talking to a friend about the weather. You will
find that Japanese frequently comment on the weather,
often as part of a greeting to someone.

atatakai (attakai)	warm
suzushii	cool
atsui	hot
samui	cold
mushiatsui	muggy
ii o-tenki	good weather
warui o-tenki	bad weather

uttōshii o-tenki	depressing (*or* oppressive) weather

Now practice Sentence Pattern 16A.

Kyō wa samui desu nē.	It's cold today, isn't it?
Kyō wa atsui desu nē.	It's hot today, isn't it?
Kyō wa mushiatsui desu nē.	It's muggy today, isn't it?
Kinō wa samukatta desu nē.	It was cold yesterday, wasn't it?
Kesa wa atsukatta desu nē.	It was hot this morning, wasn't it?
Konogoro wa atsui desu nē.	It's hot these days, isn't it?

Now practice Sentence Pattern 17A.

Kyō wa ii o-tenki desu nē.	It's good weather today, isn't it?
Konogoro wa uttōshii o-tenki desu nē.	It's depressing weather these days, isn't it?

2. Talking about food

The following list gives various adjectives that can be used to describe food.

oishii	tasty; delicious
mazui	not tasty; unappetizing
takai	expensive
yasui	inexpensive, cheap
atarashii	new; fresh
furui	old; stale
ii	good
warui	bad
atsui	hot
tsumetai	cold (to the taste or touch)
amai	sweet

karai	salty; soy-saucy; spicy
nigai	bitter
suppai	sour
ōi	large in portion
sukunai	skimpy in portion

Practice using these adjectives to describe some common foods.

oishii tonkatsu	delicious pork cutlet
atarashii o-sashimi	fresh *sashimi*
takai o-sushi	expensive *sushi*
yasui resutoran	inexpensive restaurant
furui pan	stale bread
ii bifuteki	good steak
warui o-sashimi	bad *sashimi*
mazui tempura	bad-tasting *tempura*
tsumetai sūpu	cold soup
amai kēki	sweet cake
atsui kōhii	hot coffee

Now practice some sentences.

Kore wa oishii tempura desu nē.	This is a delicious plate of *tempura,* isn't it?
Kore wa takai resutoran desu nē.	This is an expensive restaurant, isn't it?
Kore wa amai desu nē.	This is sweet, isn't it?
Kore wa ōi desu nē.	This is a lot (This is a large portion), isn't it?
Kore wa sukunai desu nē.	This is skimpy (This is a small portion), isn't it?

3. Talking about people
Practice the following phrases that describe people.

ōkii hito	a large person

chiisai hito	a small person
ii hito	a good person
warui hito	a bad person
yasashii hito	a tender person; a kind person
muzukashii hito	a fussy person; a person who is particular
omoshiroi hito	an interesting person; an amusing person
atatakai hito	a warm person
isogashii hito	a busy person

Now practice some sentences.

Tanaka-san wa ii hito desu.	Mr. Tanaka is a good person.
Yamada-san wa muzukashii hito desu.	Mr. Yamada is a fussy person.
Kazuko-san wa yasashii hito desu.	Kazuko is a kind person.
Tanaka-san wa isogashii hito desu.	Mr. Tanaka is a busy person.

4. Talking about yourself

Practice the following sentences to help you describe your feelings or situation.

Ureshii desu.	I'm happy. [or] I'm glad.
Kanashii desu.	I'm sad.
Isogashii desu.	I'm busy.
Sabishii desu.	I'm lonely.

Vocabulary Note: The above words, and most other words that describe emotions or states of being, should usually only be used in reference to yourself or when asking about someone you are talking with. Japanese hesitate to state with certainty the inner feelings that others may have.

5. Talking about things

Practice the following phrases that will help you comment on the things around you.

takai depāto	an expensive department store
yasui resutoran	an inexpensive restaurant
tōi daigaku	a distant university
chikai yūbinkyoku	a nearby post office
hiroi uchi	a spacious house
semai uchi	a cramped house
nagai kimono	a long kimono
mijikai yukata	a short *yukata* (cotton kimono)
hayai shinkansen	a fast bullet train
osoi densha	a slow electric train
tanoshii eiga	an enjoyable movie
tsumaranai eiga	a boring movie
yasashii Nihongo	easy Japanese
muzukashii Eigo	difficult English

Practice giving affirmative and negative answers to the following questions.

Sono sētā wa takai desu ka?	Is that sweater expensive?
Hai, takai desu.	Yes, it's expensive.
Iie, takaku arimasen.	No, it isn't expensive.
Kono resutoran wa ii desu ka?	Is this restaurant good?
Ē, ii desu.	Yes, it's good.
Iie, yoku arimasen.	No, it isn't good.
Anata wa isogashii desu ka?	Are you busy?
Ē, isogashii desu.	Yes, I'm busy.
Iie, isogashiku arimasen.	No, I'm not busy.

Yūbinkyoku wa tōi desu ka?	Is the post office far?
Hai, tōi desu.	Yes, it's far.
Iie, tōku arimasen.	No, it's not far.
Tōkyō Daigaku wa ōkii desu ka?	Is Tōkyō University large?
Hai, ōkii desu.	Yes, it's large.
Iie, ōkiku arimasen.	No, it isn't large.

◈ Situation 4: Using another kind of descriptive word

VOCABULARY

dame	no good
genki	healthy
heta	(be) poor at, not skillful
hima	(has) free time
jōzu	(be) good at, skillful, adept
kirai	distasteful; be disliked
kirei	pretty; clean
shinsetsu	kind
shizuka	quiet
suki	likable; be liked
suteki	wonderful
taikutsu	boring
yūmei	famous

Vocabulary Note: The words above are representative of another kind of descriptive word in Japanese. It is called the adjectival nominative. As its name implies, it is a noun that can communicate what English considers to be an adjectival meaning: "pretty," "healthy," "famous," and so on. Because it is a noun, though, it does not conjugate, and you should be careful not to mistake an adjectival nominative ending in *-i* for an adjective of the type you have just studied.

─────── **Sentence Pattern 18** ───────

ADJECTIVAL NOMINATIVE desu.	It's ADJECTIVE.
TOPIC wa / ADJECTIVAL NOMINATIVE desu.	TOPIC is ADJECTIVE.

Kirei desu.
It's pretty. [*or*] It's clean.
Suteki desu.
It's wonderful.
Yūmei desu.
It's famous.
Taikutsu desu.
It's boring. [*or*] I'm bored.
Shizuka desu.
It's quiet.
Suki desu.
I like (it).
Kirai desu.
I dislike (it).
Dame desu.
It's no good.
Jōzu desu.
(Someone) is good at (it).
Heta desu.
(Someone) is poor at (it).
Tanaka-san wa genki desu.
Mr. Tanaka is healthy.
Yamada Sensei wa hima desu.
Prof. Yamada has lots of free time.
O-tō-san wa shinsetsu desu.
Your father is kind.

Note that adjectival nominatives function here like the adjectives in Sentence Patterns 16 and 16A. Since adjectival nominatives do not conjugate, however, the past tense and the negative form are made with the appropriate forms of *desu* that you have already learned.

PAST TENSE

Kirei desu.	It is pretty.
Kirei deshita.	It was pretty.

PRESENT NEGATIVE

Kirei desu.	It is pretty.
Kirei ja arimasen.	It is not pretty.

PAST NEGATIVE

Kirei desu.	It is pretty.
Kirei ja arimasen deshita.	It was not pretty.

Sentence Pattern 19 *(facing page)* shows how the particle *na* is always placed between an adjectival nominative and the noun it modifies.

PRACTICE

1. Talking about the weather

Kyō wa suteki na o-tenki desu nē.	It's wonderful weather today, isn't it?
Kyō wa shizuka na hi desu nē.	It's a quiet day today, isn't it?

2. Talking about restaurants

Yūmei na resutoran desu.	It's a famous restaurant.
Shizuka na resutoran desu.	It's a quiet restaurant.
Suki na o-sushiya desu.	It's a *sushi* shop that I like.
Kirai na shokudō desu.	It's an eating place that I don't like.
Suehiro wa suteki na resutoran desu.	Suehiro is a wonderful restaurant.

Sentence Pattern 19

ADJECTIVAL NOMINATIVE
na NOUN desu.

TOPIC wa / ADJECTIVAL NOMI-
NATIVE na NOUN
desu.

It's a ADJECTIVE
NOUN.

TOPIC is a ADJECTIVE
NOUN.

Kirei na kōto desu.
It's a beautiful coat.

Suteki na reinkōto desu.
It's a wonderful raincoat.

Yūmei na eiga desu.
It's a famous movie.

Taikutsu na hon desu.
It's a boring book.

Shizuka na resutoran desu.
It's a quiet restaurant.

Suki na kēki desu.
It's a cake that I like.

Kirai na hito desu.
It's a person I dislike.

Dame na hito desu.
He (she) is a hopeless (no good) person.

Jōzu na Nihongo desu.
It's well-spoken Japanese.

Heta na Nihongo desu.
It's poorly spoken Japanese.

Tanaka-san wa genki na hito desu.
Mr. Tanaka is a healthy person.

Yamada Sensei wa hima na hito desu.
Prof. Yamada is a person with lots of free time.

O-tō-san wa shinsetsu na hito desu.
Your father is a very kind person.

Den-en wa yūmei na kissaten desu.	Den-en is a famous coffee shop.
Kono shokudō wa suki na shokudō desu.	This eating place is a favorite of mine.

3. Talking about yourself

Kirai desu.	I don't like (it).
Suki desu.	I like (it).
Taikutsu desu.	I am bored.
Hima desu.	I have a lot of free time.

4. Talking about people

Suteki na hito desu nē.	He (or she) is a wonderful person, isn't he (or she)?
Shinsetsu na hito desu.	He (or she) is a kind person.
Kirei na hito desu nē.	She is a pretty person, isn't she?

◈ Situation 5: Determining likes and dislikes

─────────── **Sentence Pattern 18A** ───────────

ΤOPIC (PERSON) wa / NOUN   PERSON is fond of NOUN.
  ga / suki desu.
     kirai   not fond of
     jōzu   good at
     heta   poor at

────────────

(Watakushi wa) tenisu ga suki desu.
I'm fond of tennis.
Tanaka-san wa gorufu ga kirai desu.
Mr. Tanaka is not fond of golf.
Sumisu-san wa Nihongo ga jōzu desu.
Mr. Smith is good at Japanese.
(Watakushi wa) Supeingo ga heta desu.
I'm poor at Spanish.

Note the use of *wa* and *ga*. *Wa*, as you learned, denotes the topic of the sentence—here, who is talking or being talked about. *Ga* is used here to show what that person is fond of, good at, etc.

If you use the interrogative word *nani* in place of the noun in Sentence Pattern 18A, you will be able to ask about another person's likes, dislikes, and abilities.

Sentence Pattern 18B

TOPIC (PERSON) wa /   What is PERSON fond of?
  nani ga / suki desu ka?
              kirai   not fond of?
              jōzu   good at?
              heta   poor at?

Anata wa nani ga suki desu ka?
What are you fond of?
(Watakushi wa) piano ga suki desu.
I'm fond of piano (playing).

Anata wa nani ga kirai desu ka?
What are you not fond of?
(Watakushi wa) o-sashimi ga kirai desu.
I'm not fond of *sashimi*.

Keiko-san wa nani ga jōzu desu ka?
What is Keiko good at?
Keiko-san wa o-ryōri ga jōzu desu.
Keiko is good at cooking.

Anata wa nani ga heta desu ka?
What are you poor at?
(Watakushi wa) Eigo ga heta desu.
I'm poor at English.

PRACTICE

1. Answer the following sentences using the word in parentheses.
   (a) **Anata wa nani ga suki desu ka?** *(tempura)*
   (b) **Tanaka-san wa nani ga kirai desu ka?** *(o-sake)*
   (c) **O-kā-san wa nani ga jōzu desu ka?** *(o-ryōri)*
   (d) **O-tō-san wa nani ga jōzu desu ka?** *(Eigo)*
   (e) **Anata wa nani ga heta desu ka?** *(piano)*

ANSWERS: (a) *Tempura ga suki desu.* (b) *Tanaka-san wa o-sake ga kirai desu.* (c) *Haha wa o-ryōri ga jōzu desu.* (d) *Chichi wa Eigo ga jōzu desu.* (e) *Piano ga heta desu.*

2. Put the following sentences into the negative.
   (a) **Kirei desu.**
   (b) **Kyōto e ikitai desu.**
   (c) **Omoshiroi desu.**
   (d) **Watakushi wa Nihongo ga suki desu.**
   (e) **Tanoshii eiga deshita.**
   (f) **Satō-san wa genki na hito desu.**
   (g) **Tōkyō wa shizuka desu.**
   (h) **Are wa yūbinkyoku desu.**
   (i) **Sono kamera wa yasukatta desu.**
   (j) **Yūmei na hito deshita.**

ANSWERS: (a) *Kirei ja arimasen.* (b) *Kyōto e ikitaku arimasen.* (c) *Omoshiroku arimasen.* (d) *Watakushi wa Nihongo ga suki ja arimasen.* (e) *Tanoshii eiga ja arimasen deshita.* (f) *Satō-san wa genki na hito ja arimasen.* (g) *Tōkyō wa shizuka ja arimasen.* (h) *Are wa yūbinkyoku ja arimasen.* (i) *Sono kamera wa yasuku arimasen deshita.* (j) *Yūmei na hito ja arimasen deshita.*

3. Make up your own answers to the following questions.
   (a) **Nani ga tabetai desu ka?**
   (b) **Nani ga nomitai desu ka?**
   (c) **Doko e ikitai desu ka?**
   (d) **O-kā-san wa nani ga jōzu desu ka?**
   (e) **Nani ga heta desu ka?**
   (f) **Nani ga kirai desu ka?**

POSSIBLE ANSWERS: (a) *Unagi teishoku ga tabetai desu.* (b) *Tsumetai biiru ga nomitai desu.* (c) *Kyōto e ikitai desu.* (d) *Haha wa o-ryōri ga jōzu desu.* (e) *Piano ga heta desu.* (f) *O-sashimi ga kirai desu.*

~~~~~~Sentence Patterns Covered in This Lesson~~~~~~

16. ADJECTIVE desu.
16A. TOPIC wa / ADJECTIVE desu.
17. ADJECTIVE NOUN desu.
17A. TOPIC wa / ADJECTIVE NOUN desu.
18. ADJECTIVAL NOMINATIVE desu.
      TOPIC wa / ADJECTIVAL NOMINATIVE desu.
18A. TOPIC (PERSON) wa / NOUN ga / suki desu.
                                   kirai
                                   jōzu
                                   heta
18B. TOPIC (PERSON) wa / nani ga / suki desu ka?
                                   kirai
                                   jōzu
                                   heta
19. ADJECTIVAL NOMINATIVE na NOUN desu.
      TOPIC wa / ADJECTIVAL NOMINATIVE na NOUN desu.

LESSON 6

This lesson is all about numbers and the situations in which they are most often used. Here you will be counting your money, picking up tickets at a theater or train station, buying postcards to send home, and keeping track of the time so you don't miss out on that concert, that Kabuki play, or that special tour bus headed for Kyōto. You'll also be learning about phone numbers in Japan; these will be useful when making reservations or when calling friends to say goodbye and thank them for the wonderful time you've had. Since numbers are so important, do your best to memorize the list below before studying Situation 1.

1	ichi	12	jūni
2	ni	13	jūsan
3	san	14	jūshi (jūyon)
4	shi (yo, yon)	15	jūgo
5	go	16	jūroku
6	roku	17	jūshichi (jūnana)
7	shichi (nana)	18	jūhachi
8	hachi	19	jūku (jūkyū)
9	ku (kyū)	20	nijū
10	jū	21	nijūichi
11	jūichi	30	sanjū

40	yonjū	1,000	sen
50	gojū	2,000	nisen
60	rokujū	10,000	ichiman
70	nanajū (shichijū)	20,000	niman
80	hachijū	100,000	jūman
90	kyūjū	1,000,000	hyakuman
100	hyaku		

◈ Situation 1: Handling money

The unit of Japanese currency is the yen, which in Japanese is *en*. Japanese numbers combine with the suffix *-en* to express amounts of money, just as in English we say "two dollars," "twelve dollars," etc.

VOCABULARY

o-kane	money
-en	yen (¥)
-dama	coin
satsu	bill
ikura	how much?
ichien	¥ 1
nien	¥ 2
san-en	¥ 3
*yoen	¥ 4
goen	¥ 5
rokuen	¥ 6
shichien (nanaen)	¥ 7
hachien	¥ 8
*kyūen	¥ 9
jūen	¥ 10
nijūen	¥ 20
sanjūen	¥ 30
*yonjūen	¥ 40
gojūen	¥ 50
rokujūen	¥ 60

nanajūen	￥ 70
hachijūen	￥ 80
kyūjūen	￥ 90
hyakuen	￥ 100
nihyakuen	￥ 200
sambyakuen	￥ 300
*yonhyakuen	￥ 400
gohyakuen	￥ 500
roppyakuen	￥ 600
nanahyakuen	￥ 700
happyakuen	￥ 800
*kyūhyakuen	￥ 900
sen-en	￥ 1,000
nisen-en	￥ 2,000
sanzen-en	￥ 3,000
*yonsen-en	￥ 4,000
gosen-en	￥ 5,000
rokusen-en	￥ 6,000
nanasen-en	￥ 7,000
hassen-en	￥ 8,000
*kyūsen-en	￥ 9,000
ichiman-en	￥ 10,000
niman-en	￥ 20,000
samman-en	￥ 30,000
*yomman-en	￥ 40,000
goman-en	￥ 50,000
rokuman-en	￥ 60,000
nanaman-en	￥ 70,000
hachiman-en	￥ 80,000
*kyūman-en	￥ 90,000
jūman-en	￥ 100,000
hyakuman-en	￥ 1,000,000

Vocabulary Note: An asterisk in the above list means that some forms of this number, as given in the list at the very beginning of this lesson, cannot be used for counting money. In some situations where numbers are used, however, alternate forms must be used. And sometimes either form will do. Since there are no firm rules concerning this, study carefully the usages given throughout this lesson.

Notice that the Japanese count higher numbers in units of ten thousand *(-man)*. Thus, 100,000 is *jūman*, or 10 ten-thousands, and 1,000,000 is *hyakuman*, or 100 ten-thousands.

Japanese words beginning with the numbers *san-, roku-,* and *hachi-* often show slight sound modifications. Look at the following: *sambyaku, roppyaku, happyaku, sanzen, hassen.*

Sentence Pattern 20

TOPIC wa / ikura desu ka?　　How much is TOPIC?
(TOPIC wa) / AMOUNT desu.　　It's AMOUNT.

Kore wa ikura desu ka?
How much is this?
(Sore wa) nisen-en desu.
It's ¥2,000.

Kono kamera wa ikura desu ka?
How much is this camera?
(Sore wa) samman-en desu.
It's ¥30,000.

Ano sētā wa ikura desu ka?
How much is that sweater?
(Ano sētā wa) yonsen-gohyakuen desu.
It's ¥4,500.

Sono kōto wa ikura desu ka?
How much is that coat?
(Kore wa) ichiman-nisen-en desu.
It's ¥12,000.

Note the similarity of this pattern to Sentence Pattern 8 in Lesson 3. The topic here can be a single word like *kore* or any modified noun.

When specifying amounts of money, simply combine the numbers you have learned and add the word for yen, *-en,* to the last number.

¥210	=	nihyaku-jūen
¥360	=	sambyaku-rokujūen
¥1,540	=	sen-gohyaku-yonjūen
¥3,295	=	sanzen-nihyaku-kyūjū-goen
¥12,450	=	ichiman-nisen-yonhyaku-gojūen

PRACTICE

1. Try to say the following amounts in Japanese.

(a)	¥20	(f)	¥670	(k)	¥8,625
(b)	¥90	(g)	¥1,250	(l)	¥10,500
(c)	¥100	(h)	¥2,360	(m)	¥37,899
(d)	¥350	(i)	¥3,500	(n)	¥62,355
(e)	¥445	(j)	¥6,890		

ANSWERS: (a) *nijūen* (b) *kyūjūen* (c) *hyakuen* (d) *sambyaku-gojūen* (e) *yonhyaku-yonjū-goen* (f) *roppyaku-nanajūen* (g) *sen-nihyaku-gojūen* (h) *nisen-sambyaku-rokujūen* (i) *sanzen-gohyakuen* (j) *rokusen-happyaku-kyūjūen* (k) *hassen-roppyaku-nijū-goen* (l) *ichiman-gohyakuen* (m) *samman-nanasen-happyaku-kyūjū-kyūen* (n) *roku-man-nisen-sambyaku-gojū-goen*

2. Translate.
   (a) How much is this?
   (b) How much is that radio?
   (c) How much is this stereo?
   (d) How much is the full-course dinner?

ANSWERS: (a) *Kore wa ikura desu ka?* (b) *Ano rajio wa ikura desu ka?* (c) *Kono sutereo wa ikura desu ka?* (d) *Teishoku wa ikura desu ka?*

3. Practice the following:

¥10,000 bill	**ichiman-en satsu**
¥5,000 bill	**gosen-en satsu**
¥1,000 bill	**sen-en satsu**
¥500 bill	**gohyakuen-satsu**
¥100 coin	**hyakuen-dama**
¥50 coin	**gojūen-dama**
¥10 coin	**jūen-dama**
¥5 coin	**goen-dama**
¥1 coin	**ichien-dama**

◈ **Situation 2: Buying tickets at a movie theater**

VOCABULARY

gakusei	student
kippu	ticket
kodomo	child (age 6–12)
otona	adult

———————— **Sentence Pattern 21** ————————

CATEGORY / NUMBER-**mai**   (Please give me) NUMBER
(**kudasai**).   CATEGORY (of tickets).

———————————————

Otona, ichimai (kudasai).
(Please) give me 1 adult ticket.
Kodomo, nimai (kudasai).
(Please) give me 2 children's tickets.

This sentence pattern is basically the same as Sentence
Pattern 1. Notice that *kudasai* is often omitted; when
buying tickets the important thing is to finish quickly. This
part of Japanese life is even more fast-paced than it is in
the United States.

The suffix -*mai* is what we will call a counter. A counter is a word that attaches to or follows a number to show the type or class of the item being counted. For thin, flat things, in English one would use the counter "sheets"; for example, one would say, "three sheets of typing paper." For edible things bought in bulk, the counter "pounds" is often used, as in "five pounds of potatoes" or "two pounds of flour." Japanese has many such counters. Here the counter -*mai* refers to thin, flat objects like tickets, pamphlets, or paper. Since it is obvious at the ticket window what kind of thin, flat thing you are requesting, you need not use the word *kippu* for "ticket."

First you specify the kind of ticket (adult, student, child) and then the number of tickets that you want. When buying more than one kind of ticket—for example, one ticket for an adult and one for a child—simply combine the patterns.

Otona, ichimai; kodomo, ichimai.

Notice that in Japanese the type of thing you want is specified first and then the quantity that you want—just the reverse of the way it is done in English.

PRACTICE

Try buying tickets for the following.
1. 1 adult
2. 2 students
3. 2 adults
4. 3 children, 1 adult
5. 2 adults, 1 student, 2 children
6. 1 student, 3 children

ANSWERS: 1. *Otona, ichimai.* 2. *Gakusei, nimai.* 3. *Otona, nimai.* 4. *Kodomo, sammai; otona, ichimai.* 5. *Otona, nimai; gakusei, ichimai; kodomo, nimai.* 6. *Gakusei, ichimai; kodomo, sammai.*

🔷 **Situation 3: Buying tickets at a train station**

VOCABULARY

kaisūken	coupon ticket
kembaiki	ticket-selling machine
kippu uriba	ticket window
katamichi (kippu)	one-way (ticket)
ōfuku (kippu)	round-trip (ticket)
made	to, up to

--- **Sentence Pattern 21A** ---

DESTINATION / TYPE OF TICKET / NUMBER-mai (kudasai).

(Please) give me NUMBER (of tickets) of CATEGORY to DESTINATION.

Yokohama, gakusei, ichimai.
A student ticket to Yokohama.
Shibuya, nimai.
Two tickets to Shibuya.
Kōbe, ōfuku, sammai.
Three round-trip tickets to Kōbe.
Kyōto, katamichi; otona, nimai; kodomo, ichimai.
Two adult and 1 child one-way tickets to Kyōto.
Kōbe, ōfuku, ichimai.
A round-trip ticket to Kōbe.

When buying train tickets at a ticket window, always give your destination first. Then specify the type of ticket round-trip, adult, etc.) and the number of tickets, using the counter -*mai.* If you don't specify *gakusei* or *kodomo,* the ticket seller will assume that you want an adult ticket.

PRACTICE

Translate:
1. A student ticket to Sapporo, please.
2. One (adult) round-trip ticket to Nara, please.
3. Two (adult) one-way tickets to Tōkyō, please.
4. One adult, 2 student, and 1 child round-trip tickets to Kyōto, please.
5. Two (adult) round-trip tickets to Kamakura, please.

ANSWERS: 1. *Sapporo, gakusei, ichimai (kudasai).* 2. *Nara, ōfuku, ichimai (kudasai).* 3. *Tōkyō, katamichi, nimai (kudasai).* 4. *Kyōto, ōfuku; otona, ichimai; gakusei, nimai; kodomo, ichimai (kudasai).* 5. *Kamakura, ōfuku, nimai (kudasai).*

Vocabulary Note: If you are in a train station in a large city and are not planning to travel a great distance, try buying your ticket at an automatic ticket-selling machine *(kembaiki)*. Above the machine there is usually a chart showing the fares to various destinations. Since most of these charts show the station names in Sino-Japanese characters, try, before you set out, to learn the characters used in the name of the place you are going. If you have any problems, find a station employee and ask:

DESTINATION **made ikura desu ka?**
Tōkyō Eki made ikura desu ka?
How much does it cost to Tōkyō Station?

Made means "up to" or "to." Let us suppose that the station employee tells you that the fare is ¥130. Look for a machine that sells tickets of that amount. Since these machines make change, insert the exact amount, ¥150, or ¥200. If you have to use a machine that sells tickets of more than one price, insert your coins and push the button marked ¥130.

If you plan to make the same trip often, it's cheaper to buy *kaisūken*, coupon tickets.

▣ **Situation 4: Buying stamps at a post office**

VOCABULARY

hagaki	postcard
kitte	stamp
kōkūshokan	aerogram

Sentence Pattern 21B

ITEM o / NUMBER-mai kudasai. Please give me NUMBER ITEM.

Nijūen kitte o gomai kudasai.
Please give me 5 twenty-yen stamps.
Hyaku-nijūen kitte o jūmai kudasai.
Please give me 10 one-hundred-twenty-yen stamps.
Hagaki o gomai kudasai.
Please give me 5 postcards.
Kōkūshokan o ichimai kudasai.
Please give me 1 aerogram.

Notice that the counter -*mai* is used not only for tickets but for stamps, postcards, and aerograms. The number plus -*mai* follows the particle *o*. When buying more than one kind of item you can use the particle *to,* "and."

Nijūen kitte o gomai to hagaki o jūmai kudasai.	Please give me 5 twenty-yen stamps and 10 postcards.
Kōkūshokan o jūmai to hagaki o gomai kudasai.	Please give me 10 aerograms and 5 postcards.

PRACTICE

1. Ask for the following items.
   (a)   5 postcards
   (b)   10 aerograms

(c)   5 twenty-yen stamps
(d)   20 eighty-yen stamps
(e)   4 one-hundred-twenty-yen stamps
(f)   5 eighty-yen stamps and 10 postcards
(g)   20 twenty-yen stamps and 5 aerograms

ANSWERS: (a) *Hagaki o gomai kudasai.*   (b) *Kōkūshokan o jūmai kudasai.*   (c) *Nijūen kitte o gomai kudasai.*   (d) *Hachijūen kitte o nijūmai kudasai.*   (e) *Hyaku-nijūen kitte o yommai kudasai.*   (f) *Hachijūen kitte o gomai to hagaki o jūmai kudasai.*   (g) *Nijūen kitte o nijūmai to kōkūshokan o gomai kudasai.*

2. The counter *-mai* can be used for many other items that are flat and thin: handkerchiefs, scarves, kimonos (because they become flat and thin when folded!), dishes, newspapers, sheets, blankets, and so on. In the following, notice that the *-tai desu* construction can be used in place of *kudasai.*

Kono hankachi o ichimai kudasai.	Please give me 1 of these handkerchiefs.
Kono hankachi o sammai kudasai.	Please give me 3 of these handkerchiefs.
Ano sukāfu o ichimai kudasai.	Please give me 1 of those scarves.
Ano sukāfu o nimai kudasai.	Please give me 2 of those scarves.
Kimono ga ichimai kaitai desu.	I'd like to buy 1 kimono.

◈ Situation 5: Keeping track of the time

VOCABULARY

-fun- (pun)	minutes
-han	half hour
-ji	-o'clock
ima	now
mae	before
nanji	what time?

hour	o'clock	-thirty
1	ichiji (1:00)	ichijihan (1:30)
2	niji (2:00)	nijihan (2:30)
3	sanji (3:00)	sanjihan (3:30)
4	*yoji (4:00)	*yojihan (4:30)
5	goji (5:00)	gojihan (5:30)
6	rokuji (6:00)	rokujihan (6:30)
7	shichiji (nanaji) (7:00)	shichijihan (nanajihan) (7:30)
8	hachiji (8:00)	hachijihan (8:30)
9	*kuji (9:00)	*kujihan (9:30)
10	jūji (10:00)	jūjihan (10:30)
11	jūichiji (11:00)	jūichijihan (11:30)
12	jūniji (12:00)	jūnijihan (12:30)

Vocabulary Note: An asterisk in the chart above means that the number's alternate form (as given in the list on page 106) cannot be used here.

Notice that the suffix -*han*, which means "half past the hour," is attached after the -*ji* for "o'clock." In talking about train time, a twenty-four-hour clock is used to avoid confusion.

1300	jūsanji	1900	jūkuji (jūkyūji)
1400	*jūyoji	2000	nijūji
1500	jūgoji	2100	nijūichiji
1600	jūrokuji	2200	nijūniji
1700	jūshichiji (jūnanaji)	2300	nijūsanji
1800	jūhachiji	2400	*nijūyoji

1. Finding the time

The following sentence pattern is the one most frequently used for asking the time of day.

Sentence Pattern 22

Ima / nanji desu ka?	What time is it now?
TIME desu.	It's TIME.

To give the exact number of minutes after the hour, use the numbers you have learned plus the counter *-fun*. Note the sound changes in the list below.

ippun	1 minute	**roppun**	6 minutes
nifun	2 minutes	**shichifun**	7 minutes
		(nanafun)	
sampun	3 minutes	**hachifun**	8 minutes
		(happun)	
***yompun**	4 minutes	***kyūfun**	9 minutes
gofun	5 minutes	**juppun**	10 minutes
		(jippun)	

Minutes are combined with hours to give the exact time of day.

niji	+	**gofun**	=	**niji-gofun**	
2 o'clock		5 minutes		2:05	
goji	+	**nijūgofun**	=	**goji-nijūgofun**	
5 o'clock		25 minutes		5:25	

Just as you can say "twenty before eight" instead of "7:40," Japanese sometimes use the word *mae*, "before," to make a similar statement.

shichiji	+	**yonjuppun**	=	**shichiji-yonjuppun**
7 o'clock		40 minutes		7:40 [or]
hachiji	−	**nijuppun**	=	**Hachiji nijuppun mae**
8 o'clock		20 minutes		20 minutes before 8
jūichiji	+	**gojūgofun**	=	**jūichiji-gojūgofun**
11 o'clock		55 minutes		11:55 [or]
jūniji	−	**gofun**	=	**jūniji gofun mae**
12 o'clock		5 minutes		5 minutes before 12

PRACTICE

Practice Sentence Pattern 22, answering with the following times.

1. 4:00	6. 3:15	11. 5:29	16. 6:47	21. 8:55
2. 7:00	7. 11:00	12. 1:07	17. 4:45	22. 2:30
3. 11:30	8. 9:30	13. 6:00	18. 5:31	23. 3:34
4. 6:30	9. 10:30	14. 8:30	19. 1:30	24. 10:13
5. 2:15	10. 4:36	15. 12:38	20. 7:50	25. 11:35

ANSWERS: 1. *Yoji desu.* 2. *Shichiji desu.* 3. *Jūichijihan desu.* 4. *Rokujihan desu.* 5. *Niji-jūgofun desu.* 6. *Sanji-jūgofun desu.* 7. *Jūichiji desu.* 8. *Kujihan desu.* 9. *Jūjihan desu.* 10. *Yoji-sanjū-roppun desu.* 11. *Goji-nijūkyūfun desu.* 12. *Ichiji-nanafun desu.* 13. *Rokuji desu.* 14. *Hachijihan desu.* 15. *Jūniji-sanjūhachifun desu.* 16. *Rokuji-yonjūnanafun desu.* 17. *Yoji-yonjūgofun desu.* 18. *Goji-sanjūippun desu.* 19. *Ichijihan desu.* 20. *Shichiji-gojuppun desu.* 21. *Hachiji-gojūgofun desu.* 22. *Nijihan desu.* 23. *Sanji-sanjūyompun desu.* 24. *Jūji-jūsampun desu.* 25. *Jūichiji-sanjūgofun desu.*

2. Finding out "At what time?"

Using *nanji*, "what time?" you will be able to find out what time something is going to happen.

Sentence Pattern 23

Nanji ni / NOUN ga / VERB-INFINITIVE + -tai desu ka?	At what time would you like to VERB NOUN?
Nanji ni / PLACE e / ikitai desu ka?	At what time would you like to go to PLACE?

Nanji ni gohan ga tabetai desu ka?
At what time would you like to eat?
Ichiji ni tabetai desu.
I'd like to eat at 1:00.

Nanji ni Kyōto e ikitai desu ka?
At what time would you like to go to Kyōto?
Sanji ni ikitai desu.
I'd like to go at 3:00.

Ni is used here to denote a specific time. This pattern can also be used with other verb-forms you have learned.

Nanji ni gohan o tabemashō ka?   At what time shall we eat?
Ichiji ni tabemashō.   Let's eat at 1:00.

PRACTICE

Answer the following question:
1. **Nanji ni yūbinkyoku e ikimashō ka?**
2. **Nanji ni gohan o tabemashō ka?**
3. **Nanji ni yūbinkyoku e ikitai desu ka?**

POSSIBLE ANSWERS: 1. *Shichiji ni ikimashō.* 2. *Rokujihan ni tabemashō.* 3. *Sanjihan ni ikitai desu.*

Situation 6: Understanding telephone numbers

Sentence Pattern 24

(Anata no) denwa bangō
  wa / namban desu ka?

Kyū roku ichi no kyū san
  ichi ichi desu.

What is your telephone
  number?

It's 961-9311.

Denwa bangō is "phone number." *Namban* means "what number?" A literal translation might be "What is the number of your phone number?" Though this seems repetitious in English, such phrasing is not unusual in Japanese. Note that English uses a pause to denote the hyphen break in the written number, while Japanese uses the particle *no*.

Each number should be spoken with equal stress and duration, though you may sometimes hear the numbers 2, *ni*, and 5, *go*, lengthened to *nii* and *gō*. Because *shichi* and *ichi* sound alike, *nana* is most often used for 7. The figure 0 is *zero, rei,* or *maru. Maru* can mean "circle" or "money," and seems to be the preferred word among merchants.

671-0302: **roku nana ichi no** ⎧ **zero san** ⎧ **zero ni**
          ⎨ **rei**   ⎨ **rei**
          ⎩ **maru**   ⎩ **maru**

PRACTICE

1. Practice the following telephone numbers.

(a)	771-7910	(c)	757-5411	(e)	961-9340
(b)	631-2661	(d)	261-0061	(f)	805-9471

ANSWERS: (a) *Nana nana ichi no nana kyū ichi zero* (b) *Roku san ichi no ni roku roku ichi* (c) *Nana go nana no go yon ichi ichi* (d) *Ni roku ichi no zero zero roku ichi* (e) *Kyū roku ichi no kyū san yon zero* (f) *Hachi zero go no kyū yon nana ichi*

2. Telephone numbers in rural areas usually begin with two digits.

(a)	66-3784	(c)	32-3672
(b)	23-0871	(d)	23-4838

ANSWERS: (a) *Roku roku no san nana hachi yon* (b) *Ni san no zero hachi nana ichi* (c) *San ni no san roku nana ni* (d) *Ni san no yon hachi san hachi*

~~~~~~ **Sentence Patterns Covered in This Lesson** ~~~~~~

20. TOPIC wa / ikura desu ka?
   (TOPIC wa) / AMOUNT desu.
21. CATEGORY / NUMBER-mai (kudasai).
21A. DESTINATION / TYPE OF TICKET / NUMBER-mai (kudasai).
21B. ITEM o / NUMBER-mai kudasai.
22. Ima / nanji desu ka?
   TIME desu.
23. Nanji ni / NOUN ga / VERB-INFINITIVE + -tai desu ka?
   Nanji ni / PLACE e / ikitai desu ka?
24. (Anata no) denwa bangō wa / namban desu ka?
   Kyū roku ichi no kyū san ichi ichi desu.

This lesson introduces a simple but important verb form that will enable you to describe your habits, your plans, and the things you have, or haven't, experienced in Japan. It has been designed to get you using this verb form as soon as possible, for you will use it often. The more complicated details appear at the end of the lesson in a special explanatory section; read through this section for general understanding when you come to it, but don't feel that you have to memorize it before moving on in the book. Instead, review and practice the material here often so that you feel comfortable with it.

Unit	Previous	This	Next	Every
Day	kinō	kyō	ashita	mainichi
Week	senshū	konshū	raishū	maishū
Month	sengetsu	kongetsu	raigetsu	maitsuki
Year	kyonen	kotoshi	rainen	mainen (maitoshi)
Morning	kinō no asa	kesa	ashita no asa	maiasa
Evening	kinō no ban	komban	ashita no ban	maiban
Night	kinō no yoru	kon-ya	ashita no yoru	maiyo

◈ Situation 1: Telling what you do or will do

VOCABULARY

asatte	the day after tomorrow
itsumo	always
taitei	usually
tokidoki	sometimes
yoku	frequently, often

Sentence Pattern 25

VERB-INFINITIVE + -masu.   I (will) do VERB.

Itsumo resutoran de bifuteki o tabemasu.
I always eat steak at a restaurant.
Mainichi Tōkyō e ikimasu.
I go to Tōkyō every day.
Ashita resutoran de bifuteki o tabemasu.
Tomorrow I'm going to eat steak at a restaurant.
Asatte Tōkyō e ikimasu.
I'm going to Tōkyō the day after tomorrow.

Perhaps the *-masu* verb form is the one you will be using most often in Japan. Verbs that end in *-masu* are always polite, and they indicate either present/habitual (the customary actions one engages in) or future (what will happen) time. Thus, if someone asks you, *Unagi o tabemasu ka?* he usually means "Do you eat eel?" or "Will you eat eel?"

The particle *ni* is not used with words like *ashita, raishū, itsumo,* etc. because these words do not show a specific point of time, as does *shichiji* or *goji*.

The *de* in *resutoran de* shows where the action takes place.

These are the *-masu* forms of the action verbs you have learned so far:

ikimasu	go; will go	nomimasu	drink; will drink
kaimasu	buy; will buy	shimasu	do; will do
mimasu	see; will see	tabemasu	eat; will eat

PRACTICE

Practice the following brief dialogues.

Mainichi doko de gohan o tabemasu ka?	Where do you eat every day?
Uchi de tabemasu.	I eat at home.
Taitei nani o nomimasu ka?	What do you usually drink?
Biiru o nomimasu.	I drink beer.
Tokidoki eiga e ikimasu ka?	Do you sometimes go to the movies?
Hai, ikimasu.	Yes, I do.
Komban nani o shimasu ka?	What are you going to do tonight?
Eiga o mimasu.	I will see a movie.
Komban doko de gohan o tabemasu ka?	Where are you going to eat tonight?
Resutoran de tabemasu.	I'm going to eat at a restaurant.

◈ **Situation 2: Telling what you did do**

VOCABULARY

ototoi	the day before yesterday
ototoshi	the year before last

Sentence Pattern 26

VERB-INFINITIVE + -mashita.   I did VERB.

> **Kinō sukiyaki o tabemashita.**
> I ate *sukiyaki* yesterday.
> **Ototoi Kyōto e ikimashita.**
> I went to Kyōto the day before yesterday.
> **Senshū karā terebi o kaimashita.**
> I bought a color television last week.
> **Ototoshi Kabuki o mimashita.**
> I saw a Kabuki play the year before last.
> **Kesa kōhii o nomimashita.**
> I drank coffee this morning.

The polite past tense is formed by changing -*masu* to -*mashita*. The -*mashita* form indicates actions completed in the past.

ikimasu	ikimashita	nomimasu	nomimashita
kaimasu	kaimashita	shimasu	shimashita
mimasu	mimashita	tabemasu	tabemashita

PRACTICE

1. Practice the following short dialogues.

(Anata wa) kinō nani o shimashita ka?	What did you do yesterday?
Ginza e ikimashita.	I went to the Ginza.
(Anata wa) ototoi nani o shimashita ka?	What did you do the day before yesterday?
Eiga e ikimashita.	I went to a movie.
Kinō doko de gohan o tabemashita ka?	Where did you have your meal yesterday?
Suehiro de tabemashita	I ate at Suehiro.

Nani o tabemashita ka?
Bifuteki to sarada o tabemashita.

What did you eat?
I ate a steak and salad.

Nani o mimashita ka?
Nihon no eiga o mimashita.

What did you see?
I saw a Japanese movie.

Vocabulary Note: The particle *no* is used here to make the noun *Nihon* modify the noun *eiga.*

2. In Japanese, ask the following questions of yourself and make up answers to them.

(a) What do you usually do?
(b) What are you going to do tomorrow?
(c) What are you going to do next week?
(d) What are you going to do next year?
(e) What did you do yesterday?
(f) What did you do last month?
(g) What did you buy yesterday?
(h) Where did you buy that raincoat yesterday?
(i) What did you see last night?
(j) Where did you go yesterday?
(k) What did you drink this morning?
(l) Where do you usually eat?

POSSIBLE ANSWERS: (a) *Taitei nani o shimasu ka? Tenisu o shimasu.* (b) *Ashita nani o shimasu ka? Kyōto e ikimasu.* (c) *Raishū nani o shimasu ka? Tōkyō e ikimasu.* (d) *Rainen nani o shimasu ka? Itaria e ikimasu.* (e) *Kinō nani o shimashita ka? Terebi o mimashita.* (f) *Sengetsu nani o shimashita ka? Nara e ikimashita.* (g) *Kinō nani o kaimashita ka? Sētā o kaimashita.* (h) *Kinō doko de sono reinkōto o kaimashita ka? Depāto de kaimashita.* (i) *Kinō no yoru nani o mimashita ka? Nihon no eiga o mimashita.* (j) *Kinō doko e ikimashita ka? Kyōto e ikimashita.* (k) *Kesa nani o nomimashita ka? Kōhii o nomimashita.* (l) *Taitei doko de tabemasu ka? Uchi de tabemasu.*

3. Using the following words, make up sentences about some of your regular activities.

itsumo **tokidoki** **taitei** **yoku**

EXAMPLES:

Taitei uchi de gohan o tabemasu.	I usually eat at home.
Mainichi ginkō e ikimasu.	I go to the bank every day.

4. Using the following words, make up sentences about some of your past activities.

    kinō   **sengetsu**   **ototoi**   **kyonen**   **senshū**

EXAMPLES:

Kinō sukiyaki o tabemashita.	I ate *sukiyaki* yesterday.
Senshū eiga o mimashita.	I saw a movie last week.

Situation 3: Telling what you don't or didn't do

Sentence Pattern 27

VERB-INFINITIVE + -masen.	I don't (won't) verb.
VERB-INFINITIVE + -masen deshita.	I didn't VERB.

Kyō Tōkyō e ikimasen.
I'm not going to Tōkyō today.
Kinō Tōkyō e ikimasen deshita.
I didn't go to Tōkyō yesterday.
Ashita uchi de tabemasen.
I won't eat at home tomorrow.
Kinō sukiyaki o tabemasen deshita.
I didn't eat *sukiyaki* yesterday.
Kesa kōhii o nomimasen deshita.
I didn't drink coffee this morning.

To form the polite negative present-habitual/future and the polite negative past, attach *-masen* and *-masen deshita* to the verb-infinitive.

present	past	negative	past negative
ikimasu	ikimashita	ikimasen	ikimasen deshita

present	past	negative	past negative
kaimasu	kaimashita	kaimasen	kaimasen deshita
mimasu	mimashita	mimasen	mimasen deshita
nomimasu	nomimashita	nomimasen	nomimasen deshita
shimasu	shimashita	shimasen	shimasen deshita
tabemasu	tabemashita	tabemasen	tabemasen deshita

PRACTICE

Practice the following short dialogues.

Kyō eiga e ikimasu ka?	Are you going to a movie today?
Iie, ikimasen.	No, I'm not.
Sono omoshiroi eiga o mimashita ka?	Did you see that interesting movie?
Iie, mimasen deshita.	No, I didn't.
Kinō depāto de kimono o kaimashita ka?	Did you buy a kimono at the department store yesterday?
Iie, kaimasen deshita.	No, I didn't.
Rainen Hawai e ikimasu ka?	Are you going to Hawaii next year?
Iie, ikimasen. Furansu e ikimasu.	No, I'm not. I'm going to France.
Ashita tenisu o shimasu ka?	Will you play tennis tomorrow?
Iie, shimasen. Gorufu o shimasu.	No. I will play golf.

THE JAPANESE VERB*

By now you have probably noticed several things about Japanese verbs. One, of course, is that they come at the very

---

* Do not feel that you have to memorize everything contained in this section at this time. Read through it for general understanding, and return to it for further study after completing this book.

end of the sentence. Japanese is often called a "verb-final language" for that reason. And, since -*masu* forms are always polite, you may have already guessed that each Japanese verb has a more informal form. The informal forms of the verbs you have learned so far are:

informal (dictionary form)	polite present-habitual/future (-*masu* form)
iku	ikimasu
kau	kaimasu
miru	mimasu
nomu	nomimasu
suru	shimasu
taberu	tabemasu

Other verbs that will be used in this section for demonstration purposes are:

speak	hanasu	hanashimasu
return (home)	kaeru	kaerimasu
come	kuru	kimasu
hurry	isogu	isogimasu
wait	matsu	machimasu
die	shinu	shinimasu
call	yobu	yobimasu
get off	oriru	orimasu
enter	hairu	hairimasu

The informal form of the verb is the form normally given in dictionaries, indexes, and most teaching materials (hence its name, the "dictionary form"). Although you have been cautioned about using informal language in your own speech at this point in your learning, you should be aware of these informal verb-forms. For one thing, you will often hear them spoken by others. Also, an awareness of them now will help you should you wish to continue your study of Japanese after you finish this book. But perhaps the most important reason is that many new and useful verbs that you learn while in Japan will be presented to you in this informal, dictionary form. Before you can use these verbs yourself, you need to know how to fit them into the polite patterns you have studied in this book.

In other words, you have to know how to form the verb-infinitive (what comes before *-masu, -tai desu,* and *-mashō*) from the dictionary form. This will be different depending on the kind of verb involved, for there are three different kinds of verbs in Japanese:

        (1) the vowel verb
        (2) the consonant verb
        (3) the irregular verb

1. The Vowel Verb

This verb gets its name from the fact that the verb-stem ends in a vowel. The verb-stem is used to build a number of important verb-forms. Among them is the verb-infinitive.

    (a) Vowel verbs end in *e* + *ru,* or *i* + *ru*
    (b) The verb-stem and verb-infinitive are identical: drop the final *ru* of the dictionary form

ending	dict. form	verb-stem	verb-inf.	*-masu* form
-eru	**taberu**	**tabe-**	**tabe-**	**tabemasu**
-iru	**miru**	**mi-**	**mi-**	**mimasu**

2. The Consonant Verb

This verb gets its name from the fact that the verb-stem ends in a consonant.

    (a) Consonant verbs end in *-ku, -gu, -bu, -mu, -nu;* a vowel + *ru;* a vowel + *u; -su;* or *-tsu*
    (b) For consonant verbs ending in *-ku, -gu, -bu, -mu, -nu,* a vowel + *ru,* and a vowel + *u:*
          verb-stem—drop the final *u*
          verb-infinitive—add *i* to the verb-stem

ending	dict. form	verb-stem	verb-inf.	-*masu* form
-ku	iku	ik-	iki-	ikimasu
-gu	isogu	isog-	isogi-	isogimasu
-bu	yobu	yob-	yobi-	yobimasu
-mu	nomu	nom-	nomi-	nomimasu
-nu	shinu	shin-	shini-	shinimasu
vowel+ru	kaeru	kaer-	kaeri-	kaerimasu
vowel+u	kau	ka(w)-	ka(w)i-	kaimasu

(*Note:* The *w* disappears in *kaimasu,* but appears in certain conjugations not presented in this book. Historically, *w* did exist in Japanese, and for that reason *kau* and other verbs ending in a vowel + *u* are classified as consonant verbs.)

(c) For consonant verbs ending in -*su:*
 verb-stem——drop the final *u*
 verb-infinitive——change the final *s* on the verb-stem
  to *shi*

-su	hanasu	hanas-	hanashi-	hanashimasu

(d) For consonant verbs ending in -*tsu:*
 verb-stem——drop the final *su*
 verb-infinitive——change the final *t* on the verb-stem
  to *chi*

-tsu	matsu	mat-	machi-	machimasu

Consonant verbs ending in a vowel + *ru* where this vowel is *e* or *i* can often be mistaken for vowel verbs. Simply by looking at their dictionary forms, there is no way of knowing. You can tell quite easily, though, by looking at the verb-stem or the -*masu* form. Compare the following examples.

dict. form	verb-stem	verb-inf.	-*masu* form
oriru	ori-	ori-	orimasu
hairu	hair-	hairi-	hairimasu

Oriru is a vowel verb. *Hairu* is a consonant verb.

3. The Irregular Verb

There are only two irregular verbs in Japanese. One is *suru,* "to do"; the other is *kuru,* "to come." The verb-stems of both these verbs are quite irregular and vary according to usage. Their verb-infinitives do not change, however.

dict. form	verb-inf.	*-masu* form
suru	**shi-**	**shimasu**
kuru	**ki-**	**kimasu**

~~~~~~~~~ **Sentence Patterns Covered in This Lesson** ~~~~~~~~~

25. VERB-INFINITIVE + -masu.
26. VERB-INFINITIVE + -mashita.
27. VERB-INFINITIVE + -masen.
    VERB-INFINITIVE + -masen deshita.

LESSON 8

In addition to the numbers you studied in Lesson 6, there is another set of numbers that Japanese people use to count items of irregular shape such as candy, fruit, and vegetables, and also to count age up to ten years. These numbers can combine, too, with various counters to show how many bunches, how many boxes, or how many days. With these number words plus the ones in Lesson 6, you should be able to shop or select with confidence anywhere in Japan.

◈ Situation 1: Buying fruit

VOCABULARY

Numbers:

hitotsu	1 (unit)
futatsu	2 (units)
mittsu	3
yottsu	4
itsutsu	5
muttsu	6
nanatsu	7
yattsu	8
kokonotsu	9
tō	10
hambun	one-half

ikutsu	how many (units)?

Fruits:

kudamono	fruit
kudamonoya	fruit stand
banana	banana
biwa	loquat
budō	grape
ichigo	strawberry
kaki	persimmon
mikan	tangerine
momo	peach
nashi	pear
orenji	orange
ringo	apple
sakurambo	cherries
suika	watermelon

Vocabulary Note: The numbers in the above list can only be used for counting units of ten or less. Since their common suffix -*tsu* (not used in *tō,* "ten") is itself like a counter, the numbers in the form shown above always appear by themselves. In an abbreviated form they are sometimes used with other counters; a few examples of this will be given a bit later in this lesson.

Remember that the suffix -*ya* in *kudamonoya* indicates a stand or shop. A list of the various types of stores in Japan appears in Appendix 1.

Sentence Pattern 28 below is almost identical to the one you learned in Lesson 6:

Hagaki o gomai kudasai.	Please give me 5 postcards.
Mikan o itsutsu kudasai.	Please give me 5 tangerines.

The word *hambun,* for "half," is used just like a number in this pattern.

Sentence Pattern 28

KIND OF FRUIT o / NUMBER / kudasai. Please give me NUMBER KIND OF FRUIT.

Ringo o hitotsu kudasai.
Please give me 1 apple.
Mikan o itsutsu kudasai.
Please give me 5 tangerines.
Momo o mittsu kudasai.
Please give me 3 peaches.
Suika o hambun kudasai.
Please give me half a watermelon.

PRACTICE

1. Practice the following sentences:

Ringo o hitotsu kudasai.	Please give me 1 apple.
Mikan o futatsu kudasai.	Please give me 2 tangerines.
Nashi o yottsu kudasai.	Please give me 4 pears.
Kaki o itsutsu kudasai.	Please give me 5 persimmons.
Suika o futatsu kudasai.	Please give me 2 watermelons.
Suika o hambun kudasai.	Please give me half a water-melon.

2. What do you say when you want to buy the following items at a fruit stand?

(a) 3 persimmons   (e) 7 oranges
(b) 10 tangerines   (f) 8 apples
(c) 6 peaches   (g) half a watermelon
(d) 4 pears

ANSWERS: (a) *Kaki o mittsu kudasai.* (b) *Mikan o tō kudasai.* (c) *Momo o muttsu kudasai.* (d) *Nashi o yottsu kudasai.* (e) *Orenji o nanatsu kudasai.* (f) *Ringo o yattsu kudasai.* (g) *Suika o hambun kudasai.*

◈ Situation 2: Buying vegetables

VOCABULARY

yaoya	vegetable stand
yasai	vegetable(s)
o-kyaku	customer
shujin	shop owner
ingen	string bean
jagaimo	potato
karifurawā	cauliflower
kyabetsu	cabbage
nasu	eggplant
o-negi (naganegi)	green onion, scallion
piiman	green pepper
retasu	lettuce
tamanegi	onion
tomato	tomato

1. Buying as many as you need

Vegetables are often packed loose in boxes at small vegetable shops, so you only have to buy as many as you need. Use the same pattern that you did for buying fruit.

PRACTICE

1. Practice the following sentences:

Jagaimo o mittsu to retasu o hitotsu kudasai.	Please give me 3 potatoes and 1 head of lettuce.
Tamanegi o yottsu to kyabetsu o futatsu kudasai.	Please give me 4 onions and 2 cabbages.
Nasu o yattsu to karifurawā o hitotsu kudasai.	Please give me 8 eggplants and 1 cauliflower.
Retasu o futatsu to jagaimo o kokonotsu kudasai.	Please give me 2 heads of lettuce and 9 potatoes.
Piiman o itsutsu to tomato o muttsu kudasai.	Please give me 5 green peppers and 6 tomatoes.

2. What do you say when you want to buy the following items at a vegetable stand?

(a)	6 potatoes	(e)	3 heads of lettuce
(b)	1 cauliflower	(f)	7 onions
(c)	2 cabbages	(g)	5 tomatoes
(d)	5 eggplants		

ANSWERS: (a) *Jagaimo o muttsu kudasai.* (b) *Karifurawā o hitotsu kudasai.* (c) *Kyabetsu o futatsu kudasai.* (d) *Nasu o itsutsu kudasai.* (e) *Retasu o mittsu kudasai.* (f) *Tamanegi o nanatsu kudasai.* (g) *Tomato o itsutsu kudasai.*

2. Buying bunches and boxes

Vegetables and fruit can also be piled on plates, tied in bunches, or packed in boxes for convenience. An abbreviated form of the numbers in the *hitotsu* series plus an appropriate counter is used to ask for vegetables that are displayed like this.

hito-	1	itsu-	5	kyū-	9
futa-	2	mu-	6	tō-	10
mi-	3	nana-	7		
yo-	4	ya-	8		

You will note that *kyū-* is used here instead of *kokono-*. Three counters used with these forms are:

-fusa	bunch	-yama	pile (literally, mountain)
-hako	box		

These can be used as independent words as well. When used as counters they are used in much the same way as the counter *-mai*.

Budō o mifusa kudasai.	Please give me 3 bunches of grapes.
Ichigo o futahako kudasai.	Please give me 2 boxes of strawberries.

Tamanegi o hitoyama kudasai.	Please give me 1 pile of onions.
Tomato o miyama kudasai.	Please give me 3 piles of tomatoes.

PRACTICE

1. Practice the following short sentences.

Sakurambo o hitohako kudasai.	Please give me 1 box of cherries.
Biwa o hitoyama kudasai.	Please give me 1 pile of loquats.
Banana o hitofusa kudasai.	Please give me 1 bunch of bananas.
Tomato o miyama kudasai.	Please give me 3 piles of tomatoes.

2. Express the following in Japanese.

(a)	1 bunch of bananas	(e)	1 box of cherries
(b)	1 box of strawberries	(f)	2 bunches of grapes
(c)	1 pile of onions	(g)	1 pile of persimmons
(d)	1 pile of tomatoes	(h)	1 pile of tangerines

ANSWERS: (a) *banana hitofusa* (b) *ichigo hitohako* (c) *tamanegi hitoyama* (d) *tomato hitoyama* (e) *sakurambo hitohako* (f) *budō futafusa* (g) *kaki hitoyama* (h) *mikan hitoyama*

3. Buying long and thin vegetables

If the vegetable is one that is long and thin, the counter *-hon* is used with the numbers of the *ichi* series that you learned in Lesson 6. Note the sound changes that occur.

ippon	1	**roppon**	6
nihon	2	**shichihon (nanahon)**	7
sambon	3	**hachihon (happon)**	8
yonhon	4	**kyūhon**	9
gohon	5	**juppon (jippon)**	10

Examples of vegetables that may be used with this counter are:

daikon	long white radish
gobō	burdock
kyūri	cucumber
ninjin	carrot

The counter *-hon* may also be used with objects like pens, pencils, bottles, and umbrellas—anything that is long and thin.

PRACTICE

Practice the following dialogue. Try using different prices and amounts.

CLERK:

Irasshai!   Welcome!

CUSTOMER:

Kono daikon wa ikura desu ka?   How much is this radish?

CLERK:

Ippon hyakuen desu.   It's ¥100 for 1.

CUSTOMER:

Ano tamanegi wa ikura desu ka?   How much are those onions?

CLERK:

Futatsu de gojūen desu.   They're 2 for ¥50.

CUSTOMER:

Sore wa yasui desu nē.   They're cheap, aren't
Jā, daikon o nihon to   they? Well then, give
tamanegi o futatsu kudasai.   me 2 radishes and 2
                                                             onions.

Vocabulary Note: The *de* in *futatsu de* means "for" in this idiomatic expression. Other examples:

mittsu de hyakuen	3 for ¥100
tō de sen-en	10 for ¥1,000

Jā is often used at the beginning of sentence in the same way that "well" or "well then" is used in English.

◈ **Situation 3: Counting people**

VOCABULARY

hitori	1 person	**rokunin**	6
futari	2 persons	**nananin (shichinin)**	7
sannin	3	**hachinin**	8
yonin	4	**kyūnin**	9
gonin	5	**jūnin**	10

nannin   how many persons?

iru/imasu   to exist (usually for humans and animals)

— Sentence Pattern 29 —

PLACE ni / PERSONS ga / nannin imasu ka?   How many PERSONS are there in PLACE?

(PLACE ni) / (PERSONS ga) / NUMBER + -ri (-nin) imasu.   There are NUMBER (PERSONS) (in PLACE).

Koko ni sensei ga nannin imasu ka?
How many teachers are here?
(Koko ni) sensei ga futari imasu.
There are 2 teachers here.
Ryokan ni Amerika-jin ga nannin imasu ka?
How many Americans are there in the inn?

When counting people, abbreviated forms from the *hitotsu* series are used with the counter *-ri* for one and two persons. For three or more, numbers from the *ichi* series with the counter *-nin* are used.

The verb *imasu* means "to exist" or "to be present" and is generally used only for animate beings (humans or animals). *Ni* indicates where the subject of the verb *imasu* exists. *Ga* indicates the subject, who it is that exists. In this sense, *ga* is different from *wa*, which shows who or what is being talked about.

The person-counter can also be used in the following way:

Tōkyō e nannin ikimasu ka?	How many are going to Tōkyō?
Sensei ga futari to gakusei ga rokunin ikimasu.	Two teachers and 6 students are going.

PRACTICE

Express the following in Japanese:
1. There are 2 children.
2. There are 3 adults.
3. There will be 5 students.
4. There are 4 teachers.
5. There were 6 Americans.
6. Are there 8 Japanese?

ANSWERS: 1. *Kodomo ga futari imasu.* 2. *Otona ga sannin imasu.* 3. *Gakusei ga gonin imasu.* 4. *Sensei ga yonin imasu.* 5. *Amerikajin ga rokunin imashita.* 6. *Nihonjin ga hachinin imasu ka?*

◈ Situation 4: Keeping track of the time

VOCABULARY

tsuitachi	1st day (but, *ichinichi* for "1 day")
futsuka	2nd day; 2 days
mikka	3rd day; 3 days
yokka	4th day; 4 days
itsuka	5th day; 5 days
muika	6th day; 6 days
nanoka (nanuka)	7th day; 7 days
yōka	8th day; 8 days

kokonoka	9th day; 9 days
tōka	10th day; 10 days
jūichinichi	11th day; 11 days
jūninichi	12th day; 12 days
jūsannichi	13th day; 13 days
jūyokka	14th day; 14 days
jūgonichi	15th day; 15 days
jūrokunichi	16th day; 16 days
jūshichinichi	17th day; 17 days
jūhachinichi	18th day; 18 days
jūkunichi	19th day; 19 days
hatsuka	20th day; 20 days
nijūichinichi	21st day; 21 days
nijūninichi	22nd day; 22 days
nijūsannichi	23rd day; 23 days
nijūyokka	24th day; 24 days
nijūgonichi	25th day; 25 days
nijūrokunichi	26th day; 26 days
nijūshichinichi (nijūnana-nichi)	27th day; 27 days
nijūhachinichi	28th day; 28 days
nijūkunichi	29th day; 29 days
sanjūnichi	30th day; 30 days
sanjūichinichi	31st day; 31 days
nannichi	what day? how many days?
gurai (kurai)	about, approximately
itsu	when?
gozen	A.M., in the morning
gogo	P.M., in the afternoon
au/aimasu	to meet
kakaru/kakarimasu	to require, take, involve

Vocabulary Note: You will notice that slightly variant forms of the numbers in the *hitotsu* series are used for the first to the tenth days and for one to ten days (except for one day, which has a special form). After that, the numbers in the *ichi* series plus the counter *-nichi* are used (except for the twentieth day, *hatsuka*).

1. Finding out "when"

In Lesson 6 you learned the following sentences.

Nanji ni Kyōto e ikimashō ka?	At what time shall we go to Kyōto?
Sanji ni ikimashō.	Let's go at 3:00.

Using *itsu,* "when," or *nannichi ni,* "on what day," you can construct sentences like the following.

Itsu Kyōto e ikimasu ka?	When are you going to Kyōto?
Nannichi ni Kyōto e ikimasu ka?	What day are you going to Kyōto?
Itsu aimashō ka?	When shall we meet?
Jūyokka ni aimashō.	Let's meet on the 14th.
Nannichi ni aimashō ka?	On what day shall we meet?
Tōka ni aimashō.	Let's meet on the 10th.
Itsu Amerika e ikimasu ka?	When are you going to America?
Tōka no gogo niji ni ikimasu.	I'm going at 2:00 in the afternoon on the 10th.

Ni is used here to specify a point in time. It is also used with the question word *nannichi* but not with *itsu.*

Study the word order that is used in the last example above: *tōka no gogo niji ni* (first the day, then the part of the day, then the hour). Consecutively smaller, more precise time designations are used in Japanese, while English does just the opposite (compare the Japanese with the English

translation). Think of the particle *no* in this phrase as indi-
cating "the afternoon *of* the 10th day."

PRACTICE

Practice the following short dialogues.

Itsu aimashō ka?	When shall we meet?
Yokka no jūji ni aimashō.	Let's meet at 10:00 on the 4th.
Nannichi ni Kyōto e ikimasu ka?	What day are you going to Kyōto?
Jūhachinichi ni ikimasu.	I'm going on the 18th.
Itsu ikimashō ka?	When shall we go?
Mikka no gozen jūji ni ikimashō.	Let's go at 10:00 on the morning of the 3rd.
Kokonoka ni ikimasu ka?	Are you going on the 9th?
Iie. Tōka ni ikimasu.	No, I'm going on the 10th.

2. Finding out "how long"

The days of the month can also be used to express duration of time. For example, *tōka* can mean either "the tenth
day of the month" or it can mean "a period of ten days."
The words you learned in Lesson 6 for expressing the hour,
however, can only mean the specific time of day. The
counter *-kan* is used with these words to express duration
of time in hours.

ichijikan	1 hour	**shichijikan** (**nanajikan**)	7 hours
nijikan	2 hours	**hachijikan**	8 hours
sanjikan	3 hours	**kujikan**	9 hours
***yojikan**	4 hours	**jūjikan**	10 hours
gojikan	5 hours	**jūichijikan**	11 hours
rokujikan	6 hours	**jūnijikan**	12 hours

To ask how many days or hours something will take, use

the word *gurai (kurai)*, "about" or "approximately," and a form of the verb *kakaru/kakarimasu*. (*Kakaru* has many meanings; among them are "require," "involve," "take.")

Nanjikan gurai kakarimasu ka?	About how many hours will it take?
Nijikan gurai kakarimasu.	It will take about 2 hours.
Nannichi gurai kakarimasu ka?	About how many days will it take?
Tōka gurai kakarimasu.	It will take about 10 days.

Gurai (kurai) can also be used with other verbs. For example:

Nannichi gurai Nihon ni imasu ka?	About how many days will you be in Japan?
Kyō nanjikan gurai tenisu o shimasu ka?	About how many hours will you play tennis today?

Ni is not used here because these sentences do not refer to specific points in time.

PRACTICE

Practice the following short dialogues.

Densha de Kyōto e ikimasu. Nanjikan gurai kakarimasu ka?	I'm going to Kyōto by train. About how many hours will it take?
Nijikan gurai kakarimasu.	It will take about 2 hours.
Nannichi gurai Amerika ni imasu ka?	About how many days will you be in America?
Futsuka gurai imasu.	About 2 days.
Mainichi nanjikan gurai benkyō o shimasu ka?	About how many hours a day do you study?
Mainichi sanjikan gurai benkyō o shimasu.	I study about 3 hours every day.

Densha de nanjikan gurai kakarimashita ka?	About how many hours did it take by train?
Sanjikan gurai kakarimashita.	It took about 3 hours.
Nannichi gurai Kyōto ni imashita ka?	About how many days were you in Kyōto?
Muika gurai imashita.	I was there about six days.

3. Finding out "until when"

If you want to know until what time something will happen, you can say the following:

| Nannichi made Nihon ni imasu ka? | Until what day will you be in Japan? |
| Itsu made Nihon ni imasu ka? | Until when will you be in Japan? |

Made was briefly introduced in Lesson 6, where it was used to mean "to," "up to," or "as far as."

Tōkyō Eki made ikura desu ka?

Made always fixes a limit. For example, compare:

| Nihon e ikimasu. | I'm going to Japan. (*e* denotes general direction) |
| Nihon made ikimasu. | I'm going as far as Japan. (but no farther; *made* here denotes specific or final destination) |

Thus, in answer to the question, *Nannichi (itsu) made Nihon ni imasu ka?* your response, *Jūgonichi made imasu,* means simply that you intend to stay until the 15th of the month but not beyond. Some more examples:

kuji made	until 9:00
ashita made	until tomorrow
komban made	until this evening

PRACTICE

Practice the following short dialogues.

Nannichi made Nihon ni imasu ka?	Until what day will you be in Japan?
Hatsuka made imasu.	Until the 20th.
Nanji made benkyō o shimasu ka?	Until what time will you study?
Jūji made benkyō o shimasu.	I'll study until 10:00.
Itsu made Furansu ni imashita ka?	Until when were you in France?
Hatsuka made imashita.	Until the 20th.
Itsu made tenisu o shimasu ka?	Until when will you play tennis?
Goji made tenisu o shimasu.	I'll play tennis until 5:00.

4. Naming the days, months, and seasons

VOCABULARY

Days:

Nichiyōbi	Sunday
Getsuyōbi	Monday
Kayōbi	Tuesday
Suiyōbi	Wednesday
Mokuyōbi	Thursday
Kin-yōbi	Friday
Doyōbi	Saturday
nan-yōbi	what day of the week?

Months:

Ichigatsu	January
Nigatsu	February
Sangatsu	March
Shigatsu	April
Gogatsu	May
Rokugatsu	June

Shichigatsu	July
Hachigatsu	August
Kugatsu	September
Jūgatsu	October
Jūichigatsu	November
Jūnigatsu	December
nangatsu	what month?

Seasons:

haru	spring
natsu	summer
aki	autumn, fall
fuyu	winter

Vocabulary Note: Recall that the words for this month, last month, and next month *(kongetsu, sengetsu, raigetsu)* end with *-getsu.* The names of the months end with *-gatsu,* which is slightly different. Try not to confuse them.

PRACTICE

1. Practice the seasons and months with the following sentences.

Nihon no haru wa Sangatsu to Shigatsu to Gogatsu desu.	Japanese spring is March, April, and May.
Nihon no natsu wa Rokugatsu to Shichigatsu to Hachigatsu desu.	Japanese summer is June, July, and August.
Nihon no aki wa Kugatsu to Jūgatsu to Jūichigatsu desu.	Japanese autumn is September, October, and November.
Nihon no fuyu wa Jūnigatsu to Ichigatsu to Nigatsu desu.	Japanese winter is December, January, and February.

2. Practice the following short dialogues.

Ima nangatsu desu ka?	What month is it now?
Rokugatsu desu.	It's June.
Nangatsu ni Nihon e ikimasu ka?	What month are you going to Japan?

Ichigatsu tōka ni ikimasu.	I'm going on the tenth of January.
Itsu Amerika e ikimasu ka?	When are you going to America?
Rainen Amerika e ikimasu.	I'm going to America next year.
Kyō wa nan-yōbi desu ka?	What day is it today?
Getsuyōbi desu.	It's Monday.

Such words as *kyō, kinō, kotoshi, kyonen,* and *rainen* do not require the particle *ni*. To say "on Sunday," "at eight o'clock," "in January," and the like, however, the particle *ni* is used as in *Nichiyōbi ni, hachiji ni,* and *Ichigatsu ni.*

~~~~~~~ **Sentence Patterns Covered in This Lesson** ~~~~~~~

28. KIND OF FRUIT o / NUMBER / kudasai.
29. PLACE ni / PERSONS ga / nannin imasu ka?
    (PLACE ni) / (PERSONS ga) / NUMBER- + -ri (-nin) imasu.

———— LESSON 9 ————

Japanese politeness and hospitality are renowned the world over. And Japanese people look for these qualities in others. Demonstrating good manners in your speech will make your stay in Japan more pleasant for you and your hosts. In this lesson you will learn how to produce "request" sentences or "polite imperative" sentences in Japanese. In English, requests can be made in many different ways: "Come in," "Please come in," "Do come in," "Will you come in?" "Won't you come in?"

One way to make a request in Japanese is to use what is called the "-te form" of the verb plus the word *kudasai,* "please." A detailed explanation of how to form the *-te* form appears at the end of this lesson. For now, study the *-te* forms of various verbs as they are used in Situation 1.

◈ Situation 1: Making requests and offers

The following sentence pattern provides you with one of the simplest and most commonly used patterns in Japanese. Many of the verbs in the examples are new ones for you. Study them carefully and do your best to memorize them, for they will come in very handy in your daily activities.

--- Sentence Pattern 30 ---

Dōzo / VERB -*te* FORM   Please VERB.
    kudasai.

iku/ikimasu	Dōzo itte kudasai.	Please go.
kau/kaimasu	katte	buy.
miru/mimasu	mite	look.
nomu/ nomimasu	nonde	drink.
suru/shimasu	shite	do.
taberu/tabemasu	tabete	eat.
agaru/agarimasu	agatte	come up.
hairu/hairimasu	haitte	enter.
hanasu/hanashimasu	hanashite	speak.
isogu/isogimasu	isoide	hurry.
iu (*or* yū)/iimasu	itte	say.
kaeru/kaerimasu	kaette	return.
kaku/kakimasu	kaite	write.
kiku/kikimasu	kiite	listen.
kiru/kimasu	kite	wear.
kuru/kimasu	kite	come.
matsu/machimasu	matte	wait.
miseru/misemasu	misete	show.
oshieru/oshiemasu	oshiete	teach.
yomu/yomimasu	yonde	read.

The -*te* form (-*de* in *isoide, nonde, yonde*) is most often used with a following word or phrase; in this sentence pattern, the word that follows is *kudasai*.

The -*te* forms of *iku* and *iu* and the -*te* forms of *kuru* and *kiru* are the same. Context will determine which meaning is intended.

Dōzo agatte kudasai is used when welcoming a guest to one's home. The meaning "Please come up" refers to the fact that when entering a Japanese home one removes one's shoes at the entrance and literally "steps up" into the house.

Dōzo is often used when offering something to someone else. In the examples above it makes the request warmer and perhaps more personal. When offering food or drink to someone, the following construction can be used.

Dōzo biiru o nonde kudasai.	Please have some beer.
Dōzo Hawai no kudamono o tabete kudasai.	Please have some Hawaiian fruit.

PRACTICE

Practice the following sentences. Think of them as offers to someone rather than requests.

Dōzo agatte kudasai.	Please come up (enter).
Dōzo sono kimono o kite kudasai.	Please wear that kimono.
Dōzo kono hon o yonde kudasai.	Please read this book.
Dōzo kore o mite kudasai.	Please look at this.
Dōzo Nihongo o hanashite kudasai.	Please speak Japanese.
Dōzo orenji jūsu o nonde kudasai.	Please have some orange juice.
Dōzo kiite kudasai.	Please listen.

Situation 2: Requesting things at a department store

VOCABULARY

Adjectives:

akai	red
aoi	blue
chairoi	brown
kiiroi	yellow
kuroi	black
shiroi	white

Borrowed Nouns:

beiju	beige color
gurei	gray color
guriin	green color
orenji	orange color
pinku	pink color
rabendā	lavender color
aru/arimasu	to exist (usually for inanimate things)

Vocabulary Note: Note that some color terms come in an adjective form and some in a noun form. The borrowed nouns in the above list are only a few among the many in this category. They are very popular in the cosmetic and fashion worlds of Japan, which have been strongly influenced by the West.

Sentence Pattern 31 introduces one of the most commonly used verbs in one of the most commonly used patterns. You can use it in department stores, restaurants, bookshops, and the like to find out whether the item you want is available or not.

——————— Sentence Pattern 31 ———————

COLOR NOUN ga / arimasu ka?	Do you have (Is there a COLOR NOUN?

Shiroi sētā ga arimasu ka?
Do you have a white sweater?
Akai sukāfu ga arimasu ka?
Do you have any red scarves?
Gurei no surakkusu ga arimasu ka?
Are there any gray slacks (i.e., slacks of gray color)?
Beiju no kōto ga arimasu ka?
Do you have a beige coat?

Notice that adjective color-terms can be applied to nouns directly but that noun color-terms use the particle *no* before the nouns they modify.

The verb *arimasu* is used in much the same way as *imasu,* except that it is generally used for inanimate things. The particle *ga* shows what it is that exists or is present. The particle *ni* is used to show where the item exists.

Kyōto ni chikatetsu ga arimasu ka?	Is there a subway in Kyōto?

Arimasu can also imply ownership. Thus, in the sentence *Beiju no kōto ga arimasu ka?* you might be asking whether there are beige overcoats in a store or whether a friend happens to own a beige overcoat.

PRACTICE

Practice the following short sentences.

1. **Shiroi sētā ga arimasu ka?** — Do you have a white sweater? (Are there any white sweaters?)

   Kuroi kōto ga arimasu ka? — Do you have a black coat?

   Akai sukāfu ga arimasu ka? — Do you have a red scarf?

   Kiiroi reinkōto ga arimasu ka? — Do you have a yellow raincoat?

   Chairoi sūtsu ga arimasu ka? — Do you have a brown suit?

2. **Gurei no surakkusu ga arimasu ka?** — Do you have any gray slacks?

   Pinku no sētā ga arimasu ka? — Do you have a pink sweater?

   Beiju no kōto ga arimasu ka? — Do you have a beige coat?

   Guriin no reinkōto ga arimasu ka? — Do you have a green raincoat?

When you've discovered that the item you want is available, ask to see it using the following sentence pattern.

Sentence Pattern 30A

(Kono) COLOR (no) NOUN o /   Please show me (this)
    misete kudasai.   COLOR NOUN.

Akai reinkōto o misete kudasai.
Please show me a red raincoat.
Kiiroi sētā o misete kudasai.
Please show me a yellow sweater.
Ano kuroi kōto o misete kudasai.
Please show me that black coat.
Sono aoi kimono o misete kudasai.
Please show me that blue kimono.
Guriin no reinkōto o misete kudasai.
Please show me some green raincoats.
Beiju no kōto o misete kudasai.
Please show me some beige coats.

PRACTICE

Practice the following dialogue that shows how some of the sentence patterns in this lesson are used.

CLERK:
Irasshaimase. Nani o   Welcome! What shall
sashiagemashō ka?   (can) I do for you?

CUSTOMER:
Ano kiiroi reinkōto o misete   Please show me that
kudasai.   yellow raincoat.

CLERK:
Hai, dōzo.   Here you are.

CUSTOMER:
Kore wa ikura desu ka?   How much is this?

CLERK:
Ichiman-nisen-en desu.   It's ¥12,000.

CUSTOMER:
Mō sukoshi yasui reinkōto ga   Do you have a little less
arimasu ka?   expensive one?

CLERK:
Kore wa dō desu ka?   How about this?
Ichiman-en desu.   It's ¥10,000.

CUSTOMER:
Hai. Kore o kudasai.   Yes. I'll take this.

Vocabulary Note: Another use of *dōzo* in an offering situation is shown in *Hai, dōzo. Mō sukoshi* means "a little bit more." *Dō* means "how."

◈ Situation 3: Giving directions to a taxi driver

——— Sentence Pattern 30B ———

PLACE NAME e / itte kudasai.   Please go to PLACE
PLACE NAME made / o-negai   NAME.
    shimasu.

Ginza e itte kudasai.
Please go to the Ginza.
Hikōjō made o-negai shimasu.
Please go to the airport.
Tōkyō Daigaku e itte kudasai.
Please go to Tōkyō University.

Vocabulary Note: *O-negai shimasu* is a very common phrase used in requests. It can be used instead of *kudasai* in a request like *Biiru o o-negai shimasu.* But it does not follow a verb *-te* form. *Ginza made o-negai shimasu* could be literally translated as "As far as the Ginza, please."

When speaking to a taxi driver, make sure you pronounce the place name very clearly. The best way to avoid misunderstanding is to ask a hotel clerk to write your destination in Japanese on a piece of paper that you can show to the taxi driver.

PRACTICE

Practice asking the taxi driver to take you to the following places in Tōkyō.

Ginza	Yotsuya
Shinjuku Eki	Roppongi
Tōkyō Eki	Shibuya
Narita Kūkō	Ueno Eki

◈ **Situation 4: Making sure you understand and are understood**

VOCABULARY

Chūgokugo	Chinese language
Doitsugo	German
Furansugo	French
Itariago	Italian
Roshiago	Russian
Supeingo	Spanish
mō ichido	once again
sukoshi	a little
yukkuri	slowly
wakaru/wakarimasu	understand, grasp, "get"

Vocabulary Note: The suffix *-go* means "language."

The verb *wakaru/wakarimasu* in Sentence Pattern 32 means "understand," "grasp," or "get." 'What is understood is indicated by the particle *ga*.

Sentence Pattern 32

NOUN ga / wakarimasu ka?   Do you understand NOUN?

Nihongo ga wakarimasu ka?
Do you understand Japanese?
Eigo ga wakarimasu ka?
Do you understand English?
Furansugo ga wakarimasu ka?
Do you understand French?

Recall and compare:

Tanaka-san wa tenisu ga jōzu desu.	Mr. Tanaka is good at tennis.
Sumisu-san wa Nihongo ga wakarimasu.	Mr. Smith understands Japanese.
Sumisu-san wa Nihongo o hanashimasu.	Mr. Smith speaks Japanese.

PRACTICE

Practice the following short dialogues.

Nihongo o hanashimasu ka?	Do you speak Japanese?
Sukoshi hanashimasu.	I speak very little. Please speak slowly.
Yukkuri hanashite kudasai.	
Furansugo ga wakarimasu ka?	Do you understand French?
Iie, wakarimasen. Nihongo o hanashite kudasai.	No, I don't. Please speak Japanese.
Wakarimashita ka?	Did you understand?
Iie, wakarimasen deshita.	No, I didn't. Please say it once again.
Mō ichido itte kudasai.	

◈ **Situation 5: Seeking advice**

VOCABULARY

benri (na)	convenient
dokoka	somewhere
oshieru/oshiemasu	teach, inform, tell
tokoro	place, spot

Sentence Pattern 30C

Dokoka / KIND OF PLACE   Please tell me of a KIND
o / oshiete kudasai.   OF PLACE somewhere.

Dokoka benri na kissaten o oshiete kudasai.
Please tell me of a convenient coffee shop somewhere.

Dokoka is a rather flexible word. Note the various translations in the practice section below.

Oshiete kudasai is a polite way of asking someone for information. It can also mean "please teach me," as in *Nihongo o oshiete kudasai,* "Please teach me Japanese."

PRACTICE

Practice the following short sentences and then try making up your own.

Dokoka yasui resutoran o oshiete kudasai.	Please tell me where an inexpensive restaurant is.
Dokoka ii depāto o oshiete kudasai.	Please tell me where a good department store might be.
Dokoka chikai kissaten o oshiete kudasai.	Please tell me (where I can find) a coffee shop nearby.
Dokoka oishii resutoran o oshiete kudasai.	Please tell me where a restaurant with good food is.

Dokoka benri na eki o oshiete kudasai.	Please tell me where a convenient train station is.
Dokoka shizuka na resutoran o oshiete kudasai.	Please tell me of a quiet restaurant somewhere.

◈ Situation 6: Doing what the teacher tells you

VOCABULARY

doa	door
hon	book
mado	window
namae	name
akeru/akemasu	open
shimeru/shimemasu	close

If you are in a classroom situation, you might be called upon to do some of the following.

Hon o yonde kudasai.	Please read the book.
Kore o shite kudasai.	Please do this (problem).
Mado o shimete kudasai.	Please close the window.
Doa o shimete kudasai.	Please close the door.
Mado o akete kudasai.	Please open the window.
Doa o akete kudasai.	Please open the door.
Nihongo o hanashite kudasai.	Please speak Japanese.
Nihongo o kaite kudasai.	Please write Japanese.
Namae o kaite kudasai.	Please write your name.

◈ Situation 7: Being very polite

Some Japanese words and constructions are inherently polite. The extremely polite forms that you will learn here do not differ in meaning from the polite forms that you have already learned. But they do differ in the degree of politeness that both speaker and listener attach to them. Since their proper use requires some feeling for Japanese social situations, concentrate here on understanding rather than learning to speak these forms. As a guest in Japan you will likely hear them often.

extremely polite	polite
Dōzo meshiagatte kudasai. Please eat (*or* drink).	**Dōzo tabete kudasai.** nonde
Dōzo goran kudasai. Please look.	**Dōzo mite kudasai.**
Dōzo irasshatte kudasai. Please go (*or* come).	**Dōzo itte kudasai.** kite
Dōzo nasatte kudasai. Please do (it).	**Dōzo shite kudasai.**
Dōzo o-agari kudasai. Please come up.	**Dōzo agatte kudasai.**
Dōzo o-hairi kudasai. Please come in.	**Dōzo haitte kudasai.**
Dōzo o-machi kudasai. Please wait.	**Dōzo matte kudasai.**
Dōzo o-meshi kudasai. Please wear (it).	**Dōzo kite kudasai.**
Dōzo osshatte kudasai. Please say (it).	**Dōzo itte kudasai.**

◈ **Situation 8: Going to the beauty parlor or the barber**

A beauty parlor in Japanese is called *biyōin*. Barber shops are known by various names: *rihatsuten, tokoya, sampatsu-ya,* and *bābā-shoppu. Bābā-shoppu* is most often used in Western-style hotels. Barbers can be called *riyōshi, rihatsu-shi,* or *tokoya. Riyōshi* is the word most commonly used nowadays.

VOCABULARY

heyādai	hairdye
higesori	shave

kariageru/kariagemasu	to clip the hair
katto	cutting
kōrudo	cold wave
manikyua	manicure
rezā katto	razor cut
setto	set
shampū	shampoo
suku/sukimasu	to thin the hair
suso	(trim) the ends
sutairu	style, hairstyle
chōdo	exactly
dake	only
donna	what kind of?
o-tsuri	change (money)
sebiro (uwagi)	jacket

Useful Expressions:

(Kōto o) o-azukari shimasu.	Let me take (your coat).
O-machidōsama deshita.	Thank you for waiting.
Shōshō o-machi kudasai.	Kindly wait a short while.

The following shows what might happen when you enter a barber shop or a beauty parlor. The barber or beautician will speak to you very politely (as will all people who wait on you in Japan). Learn some of the polite phrases here for recognition and practice some of the requests using words in the above vocabulary list.

BARBER (*or* BEAUTICIAN):

Irasshaimase.	Welcome!

When the chairs are occupied:

Shōshō o-machi kudasai.	Kindly wait a short while.

When it is not crowded:

Kochira e dōzo.	This way, please.

If you are wearing a coat or jacket, the barber will offer to take it and hang it up.

Kōto o o-azukari shimasu.	Let me take your ⌈coat.
Ōbā	overcoat
Uwagi	⌊jacket

Then,

Donna sutairu ni shimashō ka?	What style would you like?

Practice some answers to the above.

Shampū to setto o shite kudasai.	Please give me a set and shampoo.
Katto o shite kudasai.	Please give me a haircut.
Rezā-katto o shite kudasai.	Please do a razor cut.
Mijikaku katto o shite kudasai.	Please cut it short.
Mijikaku kariagete kudasai.	Please clip it short.
Suso dake o-negai shimasu.	Just a trim, please.
Suite kudasai.	Please thin it out.
Kōrudo o o-negai shimasu.	Please give me a cold wave.
Heyādai o o-negai shimasu.	Please dye my hair.

Vocabulary Note: The word *mijikaku* is an adverb that tells how you want your hair to be cut or clipped. It is formed from the adjective *mijikai* (learned in Lesson 5) by removing the final -*i* and adding -*ku* to the adjective stem. The addition of *arimasen* to this adverb form will produce the polite present-negative adjective form (see page 86).

When he is done, the barber will probably say something like the following.

Hai, o-machidōsama deshita. Nisen-gohyakuen itadakimasu.	Thank you for sitting (waiting) patiently. That will be ¥2,500.

(a) If you give him the exact amount he will say:

Chōdo o-azukari shimasu.   That's the correct amount.

(b) If you give him a ¥10,000 bill:

Ichiman-en o-azukari shimasu.   That's ¥10,000 and here
  Nana-sen-gohyakuen no   is your change, ¥7,500.
  o-tsuri desu.

And always, before you leave, he and the other employees will give you a hearty thank-you.

Arigatō gozaimashita!   Thank you!

THE VERB -*TE* FORM

At the end of Lesson 7 you learned how to build the -*masu* form from the dictionary form of the verb. Here you will learn how to make the -*te* form. Together, these two sections will provide you with a valuable reference should you wish to expand your usage and vocabulary while in Japan. After some use and practice, these verb forms should come quite naturally to you.

Recall that there are three types of verbs in Japanese:

1. The vowel verbs, ending in *e* or *i* + *ru*
2. The consonant verbs, ending in -*ku*, -*gu*, -*bu*, -*mu*, -*nu;* a vowel + *ru;* a vowel + *u; -su; -tsu*
3. The irregular verbs, *suru* and *kuru*

1. The Vowel Verb
  For the -*te* form, change the final *ru* into *te:*

  | -eru | taberu | tabete |
  | -iru | miru | mite |

2. The Consonant Verb
  For the -*te* form change the final:

-tsu	→	-tte	matsu	→	matte
vowel + ru		-tte	kaeru		kaette
vowel + u		vowel + -tte	kau		katte
-su		-shite	hanasu		hanashite
-ku*		-ite	kaku		kaite
-gu		-ide	isogu		isoide
-bu		-nde	yobu		yonde
-mu		-nde	nomu		nonde
-nu		-nde	shinu		shinde

3. The Irregular Verb

Memorize the -te forms of *suru* and *kuru*.

suru	shite	kuru	kite

~~~~~ Sentence Patterns Covered in This Lesson ~~~~~

30. Dōzo / VERB -*te* FORM kudasai.
30A. (Kono) COLOR (no) NOUN o / misete kudasai.
30B. PLACE NAME e / itte kudasai.
  PLACE NAME made / o-negai shimasu.
30C. Dokoka / KIND OF PLACE o / oshiete kudasai.
31. COLOR NOUN ga / arimasu ka?
32. NOUN ga / wakarimasu ka?

Iku, "go," is irregular: *itte*

LESSON 10

This lesson presents many of the polite words and phrases that the Japanese use when greeting others, when saying thank-you, when apologizing, and when being a guest or a host. Some of these are formula phrases said only at certain times; others can be used in almost any situation. Brief dialogues follow the vocabulary lists to give you some idea as to when and how these phrases are used, but the best practice situations are on the streets of any Japanese city or town. The few words you learn here will do wonders for improving your stay in Japan, and you are encouraged to use them often.

◈ Situation 1: Greeting your friends

VOCABULARY

Kochira wa Tanaka-san desu.	This is Mr. (Mrs., Miss, *or* Ms.) Tanaka.
Achira wa Tanaka-san desu.	That is Mr. Tanaka.
Hajimemashite.	How do you do?
(Watakushi wa) Ikeda desu.	I am Mr. Ikeda. (very polite)
(Watashi wa) Ikeda desu.	I am Mr. Ikeda. (polite)
(Watashi) Ikeda desu.	I am Mr. Ikeda. (informal)
Dōzo yoroshiku.	I am happy to meet you.

O-genki desu ka?	How are you?
Ikaga desu ka?	How are you?
Genki desu.	I'm fine.
Okagesama de.	I'm fine, thanks.
Aikawarazu.	As usual. Same as always.
Anata wa?	And you?
Tanaka-san wa?	And you, Mr. Tanaka?
Ohayō gozaimasu.	Good morning. (polite)
Ohayō.	Good morning. (informal)
Konnichi wa.	Good afternoon. Hi!
Komban wa.	Good evening.
O-genki de.	Be well.
O-yasumi nasai.	Good night. (polite)
O-yasumi.	Good night. (informal)
Sayōnara.	Good-by. (polite)
Sayonara.	Good-by. (informal)

Vocabulary Note: It is polite and quite common to use directional words such as *kochira* and *achira* when introducing people, as in *Kochira wa Tanaka-san desu.*

The sentence *Watashi Ikeda desu* shows that in colloquial speech the particle *wa* can be omitted.

The polite prefix *o-* in *o-genki* must be used when asking about another's health. But it should be omitted when you are speaking of your own condition, as in *Genki desu.*

1. Meeting someone for the first time

TANAKA:

Hajimemashite. Watakushi wa Tanaka desu. Dōzo yoroshiku.	How do you do? I am Mr. Tanaka. I am happy to meet you.

YAMADA:

Hajimemashite. Watakushi wa Yamada desu. Dōzo yoroshiku.	How do you do? I am Mr. Yamada. I am happy to meet you.

2. Introducing two people to each other

When being introduced to someone, Japanese like to learn not only the person's name but also his title and professional affiliation. Providing this information is the major function of the name card *(meishi)* you will often be given in Japan. It would be helpful for you to have some name cards of your own, with one side in Japanese and the other in English, giving your professional title, if any, your organization, and your position within it.

KOBAYASHI:

Tanaka-san, kochira wa Yamada-san desu.	Mr. Tanaka, this is Mr. Yamada.
Yamada-san, kochira wa Tanaka-san desu.	Mr. Yamada, this is Mr. Tanaka.

YAMADA:

Hajimemashite. Dōzo yoroshiku.	How do you do? I am happy to meet you.

TANAKA:

Hajimemashite. Dōzo yoroshiku.	How do you do? I am happy to meet you.

◙ **Situation 2: Greeting your friends** *(continued)*

VOCABULARY

Irasshaimase.	Welcome! Hello! (very polite)
Irasshai.	Welcome! Hello!
Yoku irasshaimashita.	Hello! I'm glad you could come.
Gomen kudasai.	Excuse me. (used by a visitor to attract attention)
O-jama shimasu.	I'm here. (literally, I'm going to disturb you.)
O-jama shimashita.	Excuse me for having disturbed you.

O-jama de gozaimasu ga . . .	Excuse me, but . . . (very polite; often used by service personnel)
Shibaraku deshita.	It's been a long time since I saw you last. (polite)
Shibaraku.	It's been a long time since I saw you last. (informal)
Itte mairimasu.	I'm going now (but will return). (formal)
Itte kimasu.	I'm going now (but will return). (informal)
Itte irasshai. (Itterasshai.)	Have a good time. Hurry back.
Mata irasshai.	Please come again.
Mata dōzo.	Please come again.
Tadaima.	I'm back. I've returned.
O-kaeri nasai.	Welcome back. (formal)
O-kaeri.	Welcome back. (informal)

Vocabulary Note: O-jama shimasu literally means "I'm going to disturb you," and it is often used when entering someone else's home or a room in which others are present.

Almost every person in Japan who leaves his home to go to school, to work, to the store, and so on, says, *Itte kimasu,* "I'm going now (but will return)," when he leaves. Anyone who sees him off invariably says, *Itterasshai,* "Have a good time. Hurry back" (literally, Go and please come back). When the person who has been away returns, he says, *Tadaima,* "I'm back." Those who greet him upon his return say, *O-kaeri nasai,* "Welcome home." You will hear these four expressions often in Japan.

1. Greetings on the street

Japanese often prefer to call the person with whom they are speaking by his last name instead of using *anata,* "you."

TAKAHASHI:
Yā, shibaraku.

Well, it's been a long time
since I saw you last.

KOYAMA:
Shibaraku deshita nē.
O-genki desu ka?

Yes, it's been a long time since
I saw you last. How are you?

TAKAHASHI:
Okagesama de.
Koyama-san wa?

I'm fine, thanks.
How about you?

KOYAMA:
Ē, okagesama de.

Yes, I'm fine, thanks.

2. Visiting a friend at home

YAMADA:
Gomen kudasai.

Excuse me.

MRS. TANAKA:
Hai, donata desu ka?

Yes, who is it?

YAMADA:
Yamada desu.

It's Yamada.

MRS. TANAKA:
Ā, chotto matte kudasai
[*or*] o-machi kudasai.
(Opening the door)
Irasshaimase. Dōzo, dōzo.

Yes, just a moment, please.

Welcome! Please come in.

YAMADA:
Komban wa.

Good evening.

MRS. TANAKA:
Komban wa. Sā, kochira e.

Good evening. Well, please
come this way.

3. Meeting someone on the street

TANAKA:
Konnichi wa.

Good afternoon.

YAMADA:
Ā, konnichi wa.
O-genki desu ka?

Oh, good afternoon.
How are you?

TANAKA:
 Okagesama de.   I'm fine, thanks.
  Yamada-san wa?   How about you?
YAMADA:
 Hai, okagesama de.   Yes, I'm fine, thanks.

4. Greeting the teacher

Since the relationship between a teacher and his students is considered a formal one, the polite form of greetings (for example, *ohayō gozaimasu* rather than *ohayō*) is used.

TEACHER:
 Minasan, ohayō gozaimasu.   Good morning, everyone.
STUDENTS:
 Yamada Sensei, ohayō   Good morning, Mr. Yamada.
  gozaimasu.

5. In the living room at the Tanaka's

TANAKA:
 Yā, irasshai.   Oh, welcome!
YAMADA:
 Ojama shimasu.   Excuse me (for disturbing you).
TANAKA:
 O-genki desu ka?   How are you?
YAMADA:
 Okagesama de.   I'm fine, thanks.
  Tanaka-san wa?   How about you?
TANAKA:
 Mā, mā desu.   I'm fine. (So so.)

◈ **Situation 3: Rising to the occasion**

VOCABULARY

Sumimasen.   I'm sorry. Thank you for your
         trouble.

Chotto sumimasen ga . . .   Excuse me, but . . .
Gomen nasai.   Excuse me. Pardon me.

Shitsurei shimasu.	Excuse me. (polite)
Shitsurei shimashita.	Excuse me. (referring to a past event)
Shitsurei.	Excuse me. (informal)
Dōzo.	Please. (offering something)
O-negai shimasu.	Please. (requesting something)
Dōmo arigatō gozaimasu.	Thank you very much.
Arigatō gozaimasu.	Thank you.
Arigatō gozaimashita.	Thank you. (referring to a past event)
Arigatō.	Thank you. (informal)
Dōmo.	Thanks. (informal)
Dō itashimashite.	Don't mention it.
Iie, dō itashimashite.	No, not at all. That's all right.
Dōmo. O-matase itashi-mashita.	I am sorry to have kept you waiting. (very polite)
O-machidōsama deshita.	I am sorry to have kept you waiting. (polite)
O-machidōsama.	Thank you for waiting. I'm sorry to have kept you waiting. (informal)
Shōshō, o-machi kudasai.	Just a moment, please. (polite)
Chotto matte kudasai.	Just a moment. (informal)
O-saki ni.	Excuse me for going first.
Dōzo, o-saki ni.	Please go ahead. After you.
Hai, kashikomarimashita.	As you order it, sir (madame).
Omedetō gozaimasu.	Congratulations! (polite)
Omedetō.	Congratulations! (informal)
Go-kekkon omedetō gozaimasu.	Congratulations on your marriage!
Go-kon-yaku omedetō gozaimasu.	Congratulations on your engagement!
Go-shūshoku omedetō gozaimasu.	Congratulations on your new job!

**Go-sotsugyō omedetō
gozaimasu.**

Congratulations on your graduation!

Vocabulary Note: Sumimasen can be used as an apology. It can also be used to express thanks to someone—even a waitress who brings you a pack of matches—who has done something on your behalf.

Shitsurei shimasu is often used when excusing yourself from a room. *Shitsurei shimashita* (literally, I committed a rudeness) is used as an apology for something you have done.

Hai, kashikomarimashita is used mostly by service personnel to indicate that they have understood your desires and will do their best to serve you.

1. Requesting something of your secretary
YOU:
    Kore o o-negai shimasu.   I'd like you to do this.
SECRETARY:
    Hai. (Kashikomarimashita.)   Yes, sir (ma'am, etc.).

2. Keeping a friend waiting
YOU:
    O-machidōsama deshita.   I'm sorry to have kept you waiting.

FRIEND:
    (Iie,) dō itashimashite.   No, not at all.

3. Receiving a gift
YOU:
    Dōmo arigatō gozaimasu.   Thank you very much.
FRIEND:
    Dō itashimashite.   You're welcome.

4. On the telephone
YOU (picking up the telephone):
    Moshi, moshi.   Hello? (telephone situations only)

PERSON CALLING:

    Yamada-san wa   Is Mr. Yamada there?
      irasshaimasu ka?   (*Irasshaimasu* is a polite
                                     form of *imasu*.)

YOU:

    Shōshō, o-machi kudasai.   Just a moment please.

5. Thanking your friend for helping you the day before

YOU:

    Kinō wa dōmo arigatō   Thank you very much for
      gozaimashita.   (what you did) yester-
                                     day.

FRIEND:

    Dō itashimashite.   You're welcome.

◈ Situation 4: Eating at someone else's home

VOCABULARY

Kōhii wa ikaga desu ka?	How about some coffee?
O-cha wa ikaga?	How about tea?
O-cha o mō ippai ikaga?	How about another cup of tea?
O-cha o mō ippai dōzo.	Please have another cup of tea.
Hai, itadakimasu.	Yes, thank you.
Iie, kekkō desu.	No, thank you. (I've had plenty.)
Totemo oishikatta desu.	It was very delicious.
Gochisōsama deshita.	Thank you for the food (meal).
Gochisōsama.	Thank you for the food. (informal)
O-somatsusama deshita.	It was nothing.

Vocabulary Note: In *O-cha o mō ippai ikaga?* the word *mō* means "another," and *ikaga* is a polite word for "how" or "how about." *Ippai*, "a cup," is a combination of *ichi*, "one," and *-hai*, a counter for cups or glasses (*ippai, nihai, sambai,* etc.).

When you are a guest in Japan, you should always say *Ita-*

dakimasu before eating the food—be it a meal or snack—that is offered you. After finishing, you should say *Gochisōsama deshita* to show your appreciation to the host and hostess.

1. Being served tea

HOSTESS:

Dōzo.   Please.

YOU:

Arigatō gozaimasu.   Thank you. I'll have this.
Itadakimasu.

HOSTESS:

O-cha o mō ippai ikaga?   How about another cup of
                                        tea?

YOU:

Ē, itadakimasu. . . . (when   Yes, thank you. . . .
finished) Gochisōsama deshita.   Thank you. It was very
Totemo oishikatta desu.   delicious.

2. Mrs. Tanaka brings tea and cake

MRS. TANAKA:

O-cha o dōzo.   Please have some tea.

YOU:

Dōmo arigatō gozaimasu.   Thank you. I'll have some.
Itadakimasu. Oishii kēki desu   What delicous cake!
nē.

MRS. TANAKA:

O-cha o mō ippai ikaga   How about another cup
desu ka?   of tea?

YOU:

Hā, dōmo.   Oh, thank you.

3. At the dinner table

HOSTESS:

Dōzo takusan meshiagatte   Please take plenty.
kudasai.

GUEST:

Itadakimasu.   Thank you. I'll have some.

HOSTESS:

Mō sukoshi ikaga desu ka?

How about some more (rice, sakè, etc.)?

GUEST:

Mō sukoshi itadakimasu. [*or*]
Mō kekkō desu. . . .
Gochisōsama deshita. Totemo oishikatta desu.

Yes, I'll have some more. [*or*] No, thank you, I've had plenty. . . . Thank you for the meal. It was very delicious.

HOSTESS:

O-somatsusama deshita.

It was nothing, really.

~~~~~~~~~ **Polite Situations Covered in This Lesson** ~~~~~~~~~

Situation 1: Greeting your friends
1. Meeting someone for the first time
2. Introducing two people to each other
Situation 2: Greeting your friends *(continued)*
1. Greetings on the street
2. Visiting a friend at home
3. Meeting someone on the street
4. Greeting the teacher
5. In the living room at the Tanaka's
Situation 3: Rising to the occasion
1. Requesting something of your secretary
2. Keeping a friend waiting
3. Receiving a gift
4. On the telephone
5. Thanking your friend for helping you the day before
Situation 4: Eating at someone else's home
1. Being served tea
2. Mrs. Tanaka brings tea and cake
3. At the dinner table

—— APPENDIX 1 ——

◈ Supplementary Vocabulary

Other Useful Borrowed Words:

aisu uōta	ice water
būtsu	boots
dōnatsu	doughnuts
ekonomii kurasu	economy class
erebētā	elevator
esukarētā	escalator
gasorin sutando	gasoline stand (gas station)
gitā	guitar
handobaggu	handbag
heyā doraiyā	hairdryer
kasutādo purin	custard pudding
kukkii	cookies
kurakkā	crackers
mishin	sewing machine
ōdōburu	appetizer, *hors d'oeuvre*
orugan	organ
ōtobai	motor bike
pajama	pajamas
rampu	lamp, ramp
rentakā	rent-a-car

sauna	sauna bath
shiitsu	sheets
taoru	towel
asuparagasu	asparagus
burokkori	broccoli
guriin piisu	green peas
kureson	watercress
paseri	parsley
serori	celery

Stores in Japan:

aramonoya	kitchenware store
bumbōguya	stationery shop
chūka ryōriya	Chinese restaurant
denkiya	electric appliance shop
furuhon-ya	second-hand book shop
gofukuya	kimono shop
hanaya	florist
hon-ya	book store
kaguya	furniture store
kambutsuya	dry provisions (food) store
kameraya	camera shop
kanamonoya	hardware store
kudamonoya	fruit stand or shop
kusuriya (yakkyoku)	pharmacy, drug store
kutsuya	shoe store
nikuya	meat shop, butcher
o-chaya	tea shop
o-furoya (sentō)	public bath
o-kashiya	candy shop
o-mochaya	toy store
o-mochiya	ricecake store
o-sushiya	*sushi* shop
o-tōfu-ya	bean-curd shop
o-tsukemonoya	pickle shop

pachinkoya	pinball parlor
pan-ya	bakery
ryokan (yadoya)	Japanese inn
ryōriya	restaurant, eatery
sakanaya	fish store
sakaya	liquor store, wine seller's
sentakuya	laundry; cleaner's
setomonoya	chinaware store
shashin-ya	photo studio
shichiya	pawn shop
shimbun-ya	newspaper stand
sūpāmāketto	supermarket
tabakoya	cigarette stand or shop

Kinship Terms:

For you	For others	
ani	o-nii-san	older brother
ane	o-nē-san	older sister
otōto	otōto-san	younger brother
imōto	imōto-san	younger sister
sofu	o-jii-san	grandfather
sobo	o-bā-san	grandmother
oji	oji-san	uncle
oba	oba-san	aunt
mago	o-mago-san	grandchild
oi	oigo-san	nephew
mei	meigo-san	niece
itoko	o-itoko-san	cousin

Nationalities:

Chūgokujin	Chinese
Doitsujin	German
Kankokujin	Korean
Indojin	Indian
Roshiajin	Russian

Occupations:

bengoshi	lawyer
berubōi	bell boy
biyōshi	beautician
daiku	carpenter
gakusha	scholar
geka-i	surgeon
gishi	engineer
jochū (jochū-san)	maid (in a Japanese inn)
kagakusha	scientist
kanri-nin	manager (of an apartment building)
katei kyōshi	tutor
kenchikuka	architect
kyōju	professor
o-tetsudai-san	housemaid
pōtā (akabō)	porter (red cap)
seijika	politician
sensei	teacher
ikebana no sensei	flower-arrangement teacher
o-Nō no sensei	Noh teacher
o-cha no sensei	tea-ceremony teacher
odori no sensei	Japanese-dance teacher
o-koto no sensei	koto teacher
o-shūji no sensei	calligraphy teacher
shihai-nin (manējā)	manager
shikisha	conductor (music)
shōbai-nin	merchant
shōsetsuka	novelist
sōryo (o-bō-san)	priest, monk
uētā	waiter
uētoresu	waitress

APPENDIX 2

◆ Commonly Seen Words for Recognition

Although the Japanese writing system is not studied in this book, being able to recognize the following words written in Japanese script and in Sino-Japanese characters will come in handy, since you will encounter these words frequently.

At a Station:

station	eki	駅
entrance	iriguchi	入口
exit	deguchi	出口
north exit	kita-guchi	北口
east exit	higashi-guchi	東口
south exit	minami-guchi	南口
west exit	nishi-guchi	西口
wicket (ticket gate)	kaisatsu-guchi	改札口
green ticket window (for reserved seats)	midori no madoguchi	みどりの窓口
ticket window	kippu uriba	きっぷ売場
public telephone	kōshū denwa	公衆電話
waiting room	machiai-shitsu	待合室
information desk	annaijo	案内所
bus information desk	basu annaijo	バス案内所
subway	chikatetsu	地下鉄
taxi	takushii	タクシー
boarding area	noriba	のりば
red cap	akabō	赤帽

Cities:

Tōkyō		東京
Kyōto		京都
Kamakura		鎌倉
Nara		奈良
Ōsaka		大阪

Facilities:

toilet	o-tearai	お手洗
	benjo	便所
washroom	semmenjo	洗面所
men	otoko	男
men's section of public bath	otoko-yu	男湯
women	onna	女
women's section of public bath	onna-yu	女湯

In Town:

reception desk	uketsuke	受付
police substation	kōban	交番
hospital	byōin	病院
bank	ginkō	銀行
movie theater	eigakan	映画館
dining area	shokudō	食堂
hotel	hoteru	ホテル
Japanese inn	ryokan	旅館
post office	yūbinkyoku	郵便局
in transit (taxi)	kaisō	回送
vacant (taxi)	kūsha	空車

In a Store:

shop	mise	店
escalator	esukarētā	エスカレーター
elevator	erebētā	エレベーター
sale	sēru	セール
special sale	tokubai	特売
push	osu	押す
pull	hiku	引く
yen (¥)	en	円
1	ichi	一

2	**ni**	二
3	**san**	三
4	**shi**	四
5	**go**	五
6	**roku**	六
7	**nana, shichi**	七
8	**hachi**	八
9	**kyū, ku**	九
10	**jū**	十
100	**hyaku**	百
1,000	**sen**	千
10,000	**ichiman**	一万

APPENDIX 3

◆ False Friends

English words whose meanings change after being borrowed into Japanese can give a great deal of trouble unless you are aware of how the meaning has changed. Here is a list of some of these "false friends"—words borrowed from English but having a different meaning in Japanese. English expressions marked with an asterisk are not used in idiomatic English.

Borrowed Word and Meaning in Japanese	English Word
Food:	
baikingu: smorgasbord (usually Chinese food)	Viking
saidā: soft drink similar to Seven-Up	cider
sōdā: club soda only	soda (of any type)
sunakku: (1) light meal; (2) small bar or club where drinks and light meals are served	snack
Sports:	
chansu bōru: weak return; poor shot	chance ball*
chansu mēkā: heads-up player; player who sparks his team	chance maker*
fūru bēsu: bases loaded (in baseball)	full base*
ōru sebun: "seven all" (each side has seven points)	all seven*
singuru hitto: single (in baseball)	single hit*

People:

baton gāru: baton twirler; majorette	baton girl*
bōi hanto: "pick up" a boy	boy hunt*
feminisuto: man who is kind to women	feminist
gādoman: guard or watchman (popularized by TV detective series called *Gādoman*)	guardman*
gāru hanto: "pick up" a girl	girl hunt*
haimisu: single woman aged 25–40	high miss*
ōrudo misu: old maid; spinster	old miss*
sarariiman: male white-collar worker; commuter; office worker	salaryman*
terebi tarento: TV personality or celebrity	television talent*

Home:

koppu: glass, not a cup	cup
mikisā: blender	mixer
potto: thermos bottle or jug	pot
renji: oven	kitchen range
sutōbu: heater	stove

Clothing and Fashion:

bando: belt	band
guramā: glamor girl; woman with Western figure	glamor
hai sensu: sense of fashion; wearing the "right" kind of clothing	high sense*
jampā windbreaker; half-jacket	jumper
sutairu: shape of the body; posture; bearing	style
waishatsu: dress shirt of any color	white shirt

Miscellaneous:

apāto: apartment building (usually a two-story walk-up)	apartment
depāto: department store	department
manshon: apartment building, more luxurious than an *apāto* (usually a multistory, ferroconcrete building with elevator)	mansion
pinku eiga: dirty movie	pink movie*
tabako: cigarette, pack of cigarettes (not pipe tobacco)	tobacco

Reference: T. E. Huber, "Gaikokujin no Ki ni Suru Nippongo; Imi no Kawatta Gairaigo," *Gengo Seikatsu* 7 (1971): 81–87.

APPENDIX 4

◆ Summary of Verb Conjugation

Verb Group*	Definition	Dictionary Form	Verb-Infinitive
Vowel verbs:			
eru†	eat	taberu	tabe-
-iru	see	miru	mi-
Consonant verbs:			
-ku	write	kaku	kaki-
-gu	hurry	isogu	isogi-
-bu	call	yobu	yobi-
-mu	drink	nomu	nomi-
-ru	return home	kaeru	kaeri-
vowel+**u**	buy	kau	kai-
-su	speak	hanasu	hanashi-
-tsu	wait	matsu	machi-
Irregular verbs	do	suru	shi-
	come	kuru	ki-

* Includes every type of Japanese verb except that ending in *-nu*, of which there is just one in the language: *shinu*, "to die."

† Forms presented in the book but not listed here: *tabemasen deshita, tabetai desu, tabemashō.*

Polite Pres.-Hab. Future	Polite Past	Polite Negative Present-Habitual Future	-te Form
tabemasu	tabemashita	tabemasen	tabete
mimasu	mimashita	mimasen	mite
kakimasu	kakimashita	kakimasen	kaite
isogimasu	isogimashita	isogimasen	isoide
yobimasu	yobimashita	yobimasen	yonde
nomimasu	nomimashita	nomimasen	nonde
kaerimasu	kaerimashita	kaerimasen	kaette
kaimasu	kaimashita	kaimasen	katte
hanashimasu	hanashimashita	hanashimasen	hanashite
machimasu	machimashita	machimasen	matte
shimasu	shimashita	shimasen	shite
kimasu	kimashita	kimasen	kite

GLOSSARY

The Glossary (English to Japanese) includes all words presented in Lessons 1–9 except some of the food items presented on pages 34–36. More than one Japanese word is given where appropriate. Alternative pronunciations are enclosed in brackets. For a subject-guide to vocabulary lists in the text, see pages 201–2.

abalone: *awabi*
about: *gurai [kurai]*
adult: *otona*
aerogram: *kōkūshokan*
again: *mō ichido*
airport: *hikōjō, kūkō*
aloha shirt: *aroha shatsu*
always: *itsumo*
A.M.: *gozen*
American: *Amerikajin*
American Consulate: *Amerika Ryōjikan*
American Embassy: *Amerika Taishikan*
apartment building: *apāto*
apple: *ringo*
apple pie: *appuru pai*
April: *Shigatsu*

art museum: *bijutsukan*
August: *Hachigatsu*
Australian: *Ōsutorariajin*
autumn: *aki*

bacon: *bēkon*
bad: *warui*
baggage check room: *nimotsu ichiji azukarijo*
bamboo craft: *takeseihin, takezaiku*
banana: *banana*
bank: *ginkō*
bank employee: *ginkōin*
bar: *bā*
barbershop: *rihatsuten, bābā shoppu*
bean: *ingen*

beauty salon: *biyōin*
beef curry: *biifu karē*
beefsteak: *bifuteki [biifu-sutēki]*
beef stew: *biifu shichū*
beer: *biiru*
before: *mae*
begin: *hajimeru/hajimemasu*
beige: *beiju*
beverage: *nomimono*
big: *ōkii*
bill (check): *o-kanjō*
bill (paper money): *satsu*
bitter: *nigai*
black: *kuroi*
blue: *aoi*
board (v.): *noru/norimasu*
book: *hon*
book store: *hon-ya*
boring: *tsumaranai, taikutsu (na)*
borrow: *kariru/karimasu*
bowling: *bōringu*
box: *hako*
brandy: *burandē*
bread: *pan*
brown: *chairo(i)*
brush painting: *sumie*
bullet train: *shinkansen*
bunch: *fusa*
burdock: *gobō*
businessman: *bijinesuman*
bus stop: *basu no noriba, basu no teiryūjo*
busy: *isogashii*
buy: *kau/kaimasu*

cabbage: *kyabetsu*
cake: *kēki*
call: *yobu/yobimasu*
camera: *kamera*
Canadian person: *Kanadajin*
cardigan: *kādegan*
carrot: *ninjin*
cauliflower: *karifurawā*
change (money): *o-tsuri*
change (trains): *norikaeru/norikaemasu*
cherries: *sakurambo*
chicken curry: *chikin karē*
child: *kodomo* (my); *o-ko-san* (other's)
Chinese language: *Chūgoku-go*
chocolate shake: *chokorēto sēki*
cigarettes: *tabako*
clip hair: *kariageru/kariage-masu*
clogs (wooden): *geta*
close: *shimeru/shimemasu*
coat: *kōto*
Coca-Cola: *Kokakōra*
cocktail: *kakuteru*
cocoa: *kokoa*
coffee: *kōhii*
coffee shop: *kissaten*
coin: *-dama*
coin locker: *koin rokkā*
cold (objects): *tsumetai*
cold (weather): *samui*
cold wave: *kōrudo*
color television: *karā terebi*

combination sandwich: *mik-kusu sandoitchi [mikkusu sando]*
come: *kuru/kimasu*
come (polite): *irassharu/iras-shaimasu*
come up: *agaru/agarimasu*
company president: *shachō*
conductor (train/bus): *shashō*
cooked rice: *go-han*
cooking: *o-ryōri*
cool: *suzushii*
cotton kimono: *yukata*
coupon ticket: *kaisūken*
cramped: *semai*
croquette: *korokke*
cucumber: *kyūri*
curry rice: *karē raisu*
customer: *o-kyaku*
cutlet: *katsuretsu*
cutting: *katto*

dancing: *dansu*
daughter: *musume* (my); *mu-sume-san, o-jō-san* (other's)
day: *hi*
day after tomorrow: *asatte*
day before yesterday: *ototoi*
December: *Jūnigatsu*
decide: *kimeru/kimemasu*
delicious: *oishii*
dentist: *haisha*
department store: *depāto*
depressing: *uttōshii*
die: *shinu/shinimasu*
difficult: *muzukashii*

dining room: *shokudō*
dislike: *kirai (na)*
do: *suru/shimasu*
do (polite): *nasaru/nasaimasu*
door: *doa*
dress: *doresu*
dress shirt: *waishatsu*
drink: *nomu/nomimasu*
driver: *untenshu*
drug store: *kusuriya, yak-kyoku*

early: *hayai*
easy: *yasashii*
eat: *taberu/tabemasu*
eat (polite): *meshiagaru/me-shiagarimasu*
eggplant: *nasu*
eight: *hachi*
eight (units): *yattsu*
eighteen: *jūhachi*
eighth day (eight days): *yōka*
eight hours: *hachijikan*
eight minutes: *hachifun [hap-pun]*
eight persons: *hachinin*
eighty: *hachijū*
electric train: *densha*
eleven: *jūichi*
eleven hours: *jūichijikan*
English language: *Eigo*
English person: *Igirisujin*
English tea: *o-kōcha*
enjoyable: *tanoshii*
enter: *hairu/hairimasu*
every day: *mainichi*

every evening: *maiban*
every month: *maitsuki*
every morning: *maiasa*
every night: *maiyo*
every week: *maishū*
every year: *mainen, maitoshi*
exactly: *chōdo*
exist (animate): *iru/imasu*
exist (inanimate): *aru/ari-masu*
expensive: *takai*

famous: *yūmei (na)*
fan: *sensu*
far: *tōi*
fast: *hayai*
father: *chichi* (my); *o-tō-san* (other's)
February: *Nigatsu*
fifteen: *jūgo*
fifth day (five days): *itsuka*
fifty: *gojū*
film: *fuirumu*
first day: *tsuitachi*
five: *go*
five (units): *itsutsu*
five hours: *gojikan*
five minutes: *gofun*
five persons: *gonin*
folding screens: *byōbu*
folk craft: *mingeihin*
forty: *yonjū*
four: *shi, yo, yon*
four (units): *yottsu*
four hours: *yojikan*
four minutes: *yompun*
four persons: *yonin*

fourteen: *jūshi, jūyon*
fourth day (four days): *yokka*
free (time): *hima (na)*
French language: *Furansugo*
French person: *Furansujin*
Friday: *Kin-yōbi*
fruit: *kudamono*
fruit stand: *kudamonoya*

German language: *Doitsugo*
get off: *oriru/orimasu*
get on: *noru/norimasu*
gin fizz: *jin fuizu*
give: *ageru/agemasu*
give (polite): *sashiageru/sashiagemasu*
give (me, please): *kudasai*
glad: *ureshii*
go: *iku/ikimasu*
golf: *gorufu*
good: *ii*
go out: *dekakeru/dekake-masu*
grape: *budō*
gray: *gurei*
green: *guriin*
green onion: *o-negi, naganegi*
green pepper: *piiman*
grill: *guriru*

hairdye: *heyādai*
half: *hambun*
ham: *hamu*
hamburger: *hambāgā*
ham sandwich: *hamu sando-itchi* [*hamu sando*]
handkerchief: *hankachi*

happi coat: *happi*
hard (texture): *katai*
Hawaiian person: *Hawaijin*
he: *kare*
healthy: *genki (na)*
here: *koko*
home: *uchi, ie*
hospital: *byōin*
hostess: *hosutesu*
hot: *atsui*
hotel: *hoteru*
hotel dining room: *hoteru no shokudō*
how many (units)?: *ikutsu*
how many days?: *nannichi*
how many hours?: *nanjikan*
how many persons?: *nannin*
how much?: *ikura*
hundred: *hyaku*
hundred thousand: *jūman*
hurry: *isogu/isogimasu*
husband: *shujin* (my); *go-shujin* (other's)

I: *watashi* (informal); *watakushi* (polite)
ice coffee: *aisu kōhii*
ice cream: *aisukuriimu*
ice cream soda: *aisukuriimu sōda*
inexpensive: *yasui*
information desk: *annaijo*
interesting: *omoshiroi*
Italian language: *Itariago*
Italian person: *Itariajin*

jacket: *sebiro, uwagi*

January: *Ichigatsu*
Japan: *Nihon [Nippon]*
Japanese inn: *ryokan*
Japanese language: *Nihongo [Nippongo]*
Japanese-style food: *washoku*
Japanese tea: *o-cha*
Japanese wooden doll: *ko-keshi*
juice: *jūsu*
July: *Shichigatsu*
June: *Rokugatsu*

Kabuki play: *Kabuki*
kimono: *kimono*
kind: *shinsetsu (na)*

last evening: *kinō no ban*
last month: *sengetsu*
last night: *kinō no yoru*
last week: *senshū*
last year: *kyonen*
lavender: *rabendā*
learn: *narau/naraimasu*
leave: *deru/demasu*
lend: *kasu/kashimasu*
lettuce: *retasu*
library: *toshokan*
likable: *suki (na)*
listen: *kiku/kikimasu*
(a) little: *sukoshi*
lonely: *sabishii*
long: *nagai*
loquat: *biwa*
low (height): *hikui*

mail: *dasu/dashimasu*

make (a telephone call): *(denwa o) kakeru/kakemasu*
make (cook): *tsukuru/tsukurimasu*
manicure: *manikyua*
March: *Sangatsu*
marriage: *kekkon*
May: *Gogatsu*
meal: *shokuji*
medical doctor: *isha; o-isha-san* (in addressing)
meet: *au/aimasu*
milk: *miruku*
million: *hyakuman*
minutes: *-fun [-pun]*
Monday: *Getsuyōbi*
money: *o-kane*
mother: *haha* (my); *o-kā-san* (other's)
movie: *eiga*
movie theater: *eigakan*
muggy: *mushiatsui*

name: *namae*
near: *chikai*
necktie: *nekutai*
new: *atarashii*
next month: *raigetsu*
next week: *raishū*
next year: *rainen*
nine: *ku, kyū*
nine (units): *kokonotsu*
nine hours: *kujikan*
nine minutes: *kyūfun*
nine persons: *kyūnin*
nineteen: *jūku, jūkyū*
ninety: *kyūjū*

ninth day (nine days): *kokonoka*
no: *iie*
Noh play: *Nō*
noodles: *soba, udon*
November: *Jūichigatsu*
now: *ima*
nurse: *kangofu; kangofu-san* (in addressing)

-o'clock: *-ji*
October: *Jūgatsu*
octopus: *tako*
often: *yoku*
old (things): *furui*
omelet: *omuretsu*
one: *ichi*
one (unit): *hitotsu*
one-course meal: *ippin ryōri*
one day: *ichinichi*
one hour: *ichijikan*
one minute: *ippun*
one person: *hitori*
one-way (ticket): *katamichi (kippu)*
onion: *tamanegi*
only: *dake*
open: *akeru/akemasu*
orange: *orenji*
orange (color): *orenji*
orange juice: *orenji jūsu*
over that way: *achira*
over there: *asoko*

pay: *harau/haraimasu*
peach: *momo*
pear: *nashi*

pearl: *shinju*
persimmon: *kaki*
person: *hito*
phone number: *denwa bangō*
photo studio: *shashin-ya*
piano: *piano*
pie: *pai*
pile (mountain): *yama*
pink: *pinku*
please (offering something):
  dōzo
plentiful: *ōi*
P.M.: *gogo*
policeman: *keikan, o-mawa-ri-san*
police substation: *kōban, kō-bansho*
pork cutlet: *tonkatsu*
postcard: *hagaki*
post office: *yūbinkyoku*
potato: *jagaimo*
pottery: *yakimono*
practice: *renshū*
pretty: *kirei (na)*
public telephone: *kōshū den-wa*
puppet play: *Bunraku*

quiet: *shizuka (na)*

radio: *rajio*
radish: *daikon*
raincoat: *reinkōto [renkōto]*
razor cut: *rezā katto*
read: *yomu/yomimasu*
record: *rekōdo*
red: *akai*

require (time): *kakaru/kaka-rimasu*
rest: *yasumu/yasumimasu*
return (things): *kaesu/kaeshi-masu*
return home: *kaeru/kaeri-masu*
roast beef: *rōsuto biifu*
round-trip ticket: *ōfuku (kippu)*
rum: *ramu*
Russian language: *Roshiago*

sad: *kanashii*
sakè: *o-sake*
salad: *sarada*
salmon roe: *ikura*
salty: *karai*
sandals (Japanese-style): *zōri*
sandwich: *sandoitchi [sando]*
sash: *obi*
Saturday: *Doyōbi*
sausage: *sōsēji*
say: *iu [yū]/iimasu*
say (polite): *ossharu/osshai-masu*
scarce: *sukunai*
scarf: *sukāfu*
school: *gakkō*
Scotch whiskey: *Sukotchi uisukii*
sea urchin: *uni*
second day (two days): *futsu-ka*
secretary: *hisho*
see: *miru/mimasu*
send: *okuru/okurimasu*

September: *Kugatsu*
set: *setto*
seven: *shichi, nana*
seven (units): *nanatsu*
seven hours: *shichijikan*
seven minutes: *shichifun, nanafun*
seven persons: *nananin, shichinin*
seventeen: *jūshichi, jūnana*
seventh day (seven days): *nanoka [nanuka]*
seventy: *nanajū, shichijū*
shampoo: *shampū*
shave: *higesori*
she: *kanojo*
shop owner: *shujin*
short: *mijikai*
show: *miseru/misemasu*
shrimp: *ebi*
shrimp curry: *shurimpu karē*
shrine: *jinja*
sightseeing: *kembutsu*
sit: *suwaru/suwarimasu*
six: *roku*
six (units): *muttsu*
six hours: *rokujikan*
six minutes: *roppun*
six persons: *rokunin*
sixteen: *jūroku*
sixth day (six days): *muika*
sixty: *rokujū*
skating: *sukēto*
skiing: *sukii*
skillful: *jōzu (na)*
skirt: *sukāto*

slacks: *surakkusu*
sleep, go to bed: *neru/nemasu*
slow: *osoi*
slowly: *yukkuri*
small: *chiisai*
soda: *sōda*
soft: *yawarakai*
sometimes: *tokidoki*
son: *musuko* (my); *musukosan* (other's)
soup: *sūpu*
sour: *suppai*
spacious: *hiroi*
Spanish language: *Supeingo*
Spanish person: *Supeinjin*
sports shirt: *supōtsu shatsu*
spring: *haru*
squid: *ika*
stamp: *kitte*
station: *eki*
station employee: *eki-in*
station store: *eki no baiten*
stereo: *sutereo*
stop: *yameru/yamemasu*
store clerk: *ten-in*
straight (liquor): *sutorēto de*
strawberry: *ichigo*
student: *gakusei*
study: *benkyō*
style: *sutairu*
subway station: *chikatetsu no eki, chikatetsu no noriba*
suit: *sūtsu*
summer: *natsu*
Sunday: *Nichiyōbi*
sweater: *sētā*

sweet: *amai*
sword: *katana*

talk: *hanasu/hanashimasu*
tangerine: *mikan*
tape recorder: *tēpu rekōdā*
taxi stand: *takushii noriba*
teach: *oshieru/oshiemasu*
teacher: *sensei*
telephone operator: *kōkan-shu, denwa no kōkanshu*
television set: *terebi*
ten: *jū*
ten (units): *tō*
ten hours: *jūjikan*
ten minutes: *juppun [jippun]*
tennis: *tenisu*
ten persons: *jūnin*
tenth day (ten days): *tōka*
ten thousand: *ichiman*
there: *soko*
these days: *konogoro*
thin (the hair): (kami o) *suku/sukimasu*
think: *kangaeru/kangaemasu*
third day (three days): *mikka*
thirteen: *jūsan*
thirty: *sanjū*
this: *kore*
this evening: *komban*
this month: *kongetsu*
this morning: *kesa*
this way: *kochira*
this week: *konshū*
this year: *kotoshi*
thousand: *sen*

three: *san*
three (units): *mittsu*
three hours: *sanjikan*
three minutes: *sampun*
three persons: *sannin*
Thursday: *Mokuyōbi*
ticket: *kippu*
ticket-selling machine: *kem-baiki*
ticket window: *kippu uriba*
to, as far as: *made*
today: *kyō*
toilet: *o-tearai*
tomato: *tomato*
tomato juice: *tomato jūsu*
tomorrow: *ashita*
tomorrow evening: *ashita no ban*
tomorrow morning: *ashita no asa*
tomorrow night: *ashita no yoru*
tonight: *kon-ya*
toward you: *sochira*
travel: *ryokō*
trim: *suso (dake karu)*
trousers: *zubon*
Tuesday: *Kayōbi*
tuna: *maguro*
tuna (belly flesh): *toro*
turn: *magaru/magarimasu*
twelve: *jūni*
twelve hours: *jūnijikan*
twentieth day (twenty days): *hatsuka*
twenty: *nijū*

twenty-thousand: *niman*
two: *ni*
two (units): *futatsu*
two hours: *nijikan*
two minutes: *nifun*
two persons: *futari*
two thousand: *nisen*

unappetizing: *mazui*
underpants: *pantsu*
undershirt: *shatsu*
understand: *wakaru/wakari-masu*
university: *daigaku*
unskilled: *heta (na)*
useless: *dame (na)*
usually: *taitei*

vegetable: *yasai*
vegetable stand: *yaoya*
vodka: *uokka*

wait: *matsu/machimasu*
walk: *aruku/arukimasu*
(a) walk: *sampo*
warm: *atatakai [attakai]*
wash: *arau/araimasu*
water: *o-mizu*
(liquor with) water and ice: *mizuwari de*
watermelon: *suika*
wear: *kiru/kimasu*
weather: *o-tenki*
Wednesday: *Suiyōbi*
Western-style food: *yōshoku*
what: *nan(i)*

what day?: *nannichi*
what day of the week?: *nan-yōbi*
what kind of?: *donna*
what month?: *nangatsu*
what number? *namban*
what time?: *nanji*
wheat noodles: *soba*
when?: *itsu*
where?: *doko*
which?: *dore*
which way?: *dochira*
whiskey: *uisukii*
whiskey sour: *uisukii sawā*
white: *shiroi*
white-collar employee: *sara-riiman*
wife: *kanai* (my); *oku-san* (other's)
window: *mado*
winter: *fuyu*
wonderful: *suteki (na)*
woodblock print: *hanga*
write: *kaku/kakimasu*

year before last: *ototoshi*
yellow: *kiiroi*
yen: *-en*
yes: *hai, ē*
yesterday: *kinō*
yesterday morning: *kinō no asa*
you: *anata*
young: *wakai*

zero: *rei, maru, zero*

INDEXES

Grammar Discussions

adjectival nominatives, 98–105

adjectives, 81–98
  for colors, 152–54
  conjugation, 85–88

adverbs, 163
  of frequency, 123
  of time, 83, 122–23, 125

borrowed words, 23, 24, 26–27, 28, 30, 153

consonants, 19–20
consonant verbs, 130–31
copula
  desu, 39, 56, 60, 84, 86, 100
  deshita, 87, 100
counters
  -en (yen), 107–10
  -fun (minutes), 118
  -fusa (bunch), 137
  -hako (box), 137
  -han (half past the hour), 117

-hon (long, thin object), 138–39

-ji (o'clock), 117

-ka (day), 141–43

-kan (hour), 144

-mai (thin, flat object), 111–12, 113, 115, 116, 134

-nen (year), 122

-nichi (day), 141–43

-nin/*-ri* (person), 140–41

-tsu (general unit), 133–34, 137, 142

-yama (pile), 137

demonstratives
  kore, sore, are, dore, 31–32, 52, 56, 59–60, 62–64, 76
  other forms (*kono, koko, kochira*, etc.), 31–32, 50, 55, 56, 77

desu. See copula

double consonants, 19, 21

honorifics, 160–61

irregular verbs, 130, 132, 164–65

long vowels, 17–18, 20

nē, 84, 85
negatives, 44–45, 62–63, 64–65, 68–69, 86–87, 91, 100, 127–28
numerical systems, 106–10, 117, 118, 133–34, 137, 138, 140, 141–43

particles
  de (for), 139
  de (manner), 27
  de (place of action), 123
  e (direction), 38–39
  ga (object marker), 38–39, 74, 103, 157–58
  ga (subject marker), 140–41, 153–54
  made (up to), 114, 146, 156
  na (with adj. nom), 100
  ni (place), 140–41, 154
  ni (point of time), 119–20, 123, 143, 145, 149
  no (of), 68, 126, 143–44, 154
  o (object marker), 25, 27, 73–74, 115, 158
  to (and), 28–29, 115, 141
  wa (topic marker), 55, 89, 103, 141, 167

personal pronouns, 66–67
phrasing, 21–22
polite prefixes, 37, 39, 167
pronunciation, 17–22, 37, 54, 60, 109

questions, 41–42, 46–47, 48, 50, 55, 59–60, 62–63, 68–69, 75–77, 103, 109, 114, 117, 119, 120, 140–41, 143, 144–45, 146, 153–54, 155, 158

requests, 25, 29, 31, 111–12, 113, 115, 135, 137–38, 151–52, 153–54, 155, 156–57, 159, 160–61, 173

short vowels, 17, 18
suffixes
  -chan (names), 67
  -dai (university), 59
  -gatsu (month), 147–48
  -getsu (month), 122, 148
  -go (language), 157
  -ji (temple), 59
  -jin (person), 66
  -jō (castle), 59
  -kai (sea), 59
  -ko (lake), 59
  -san (names), 67
  -sensei (teacher, doctor), 67
  -shū (week), 122
  -ya (shop, stand), 54, 134
  -yōbi (day of the week), 147
syllables, 18–19, 20–21

verbs, 37–39, 43, 123–25,
127–32
  dictionary forms, 129–30
  infinitive, 38–39, 72, 130–
    32
  -mashō forms (Let's . . .),
    72–74, 75–77, 79–80
  -masu forms, 123–24, 125,
    127–28, 129–30
  stem, 130–32

-tai forms (desire), 37–39,
  42–43, 44–45, 46–48,
  50, 72, 116
-te forms, 150–51, 164–65
vowel verbs, 130, 164

yes and no answers, 41–43,
  44–45, 62–63, 64–65,
  68–69, 76

◈ Vocabulary Lists

adjectival nominatives, 98,
  159
adjectives, 81–83, 152
adverbs, 123, 157, 159, 162
  of time, 83, 116, 122, 123,
    124, 142
arts and handicrafts, 36–37

beauty parlor/barber shop
  terms, 162
borrowed words, 24, 26–27,
  28, 30, 153

clothing, 36
colors, 152–53
common nouns, 30, 53–54,
  66, 71–72, 83, 111, 113,
  115, 134, 136, 137, 159,
  160, 161–62
  used with *suru*, 71–72, 74

days, 141–42, 147

entertainment, 36

food and beverages
  foreign (borrowed), 24,
    26–27, 28
  Japanese, 34–36, 134, 136,
    139
  words for talking about, 94

kinship terms, 65

languages, 83, 157

money, 107–8
months, 147–48

nationalities, 66
numbers, 106–7

numbers *(cont'd)*
  for counting things and people, 133, 137, 138, 140, 144

occupations, 66

personal pronouns, 66, 67
places
  around town, 53–54
  proper names, 59
polite words and phrases, 162, 166–67, 168–69, 171–73, 174

seasons, 148
sports and games, 71
stores and shops, 53–54, 134, 136

-*te* forms, 151
time, 116–17, 118, 141–42, 144

verbs, 79–80, 129, 140, 142, 151, 153, 157, 159, 160, 162

weather, 93–94